C000225434

Philosop

Being while Existing

Editor
Timothy Williams

Cover Design and Illustration by
Hannah Wood

Terry Williams

Produced by Terry Williams
Published by Anchorprint Group Ltd
First Printed 2008

Copyright © Terry Williams 2008

Printed by Anchorprint Group Ltd, Leicester.
Cover design and illustration by Hannah Wood

British Library Cataloguing in Publication Data

Data Available
ISBN 978-0-9556367-3-8

In recognition of love and affection, practiced by my mother and father, Stella of Redcliffe, and the monastic community, in their devotion to others at large, and bequeathed to me. This assuring legacy, derived from awareness of the truth of perpetual being, is now the inheritance of my students, my children and all our benevolent fellows.

Live as if to die tomorrow, but learn to live as if forever.

Gandhi

The world of being is unchangeable while the world of existence is fleeting.

Bertrand Russell

Just as science can demonstrate that matter and energy are interchangeable, and have a sense of equivalence, so does reasoning reveal a similar sense of equivalence and interchangeability between the happening or *phenomenon* of a thing, (including personhood), and the *truth* authorising it.

Then again, as light is equivalent to a given fragmentary quantity of mass in the sun, a thing or event has equivalence as a fragment of truth. In the event of individual human living and existing, while the *truth of being* must be there for life to *be* of reality, a fragment of truth, the individual, moves concurrently with physical existence. When the individual's life ends however, it is imperative that whatever is truth of it transfers in entirety from *existence* within physics to *being* of *unending truth* in metaphysics. This involves no change of identity for what is of truth is unchanging and endless, while what *lives* is simply an expression of this.

There cannot be actuality without truth. No thing can happen without unchanging truth. There is no event without truth substance, no phenomenon without significance, no body manifest or disclosed without authentication and provenance of truth substance. This is universally presupposed as necessary premise from which all codes of civilisation spring. Value is thus intrinsic to all individual human life.

The required premise for anything that can ever be, clearly, is an *object of abstraction*, truth, (a feature of metaphysic substance), by which all things have any claim of credentials and authenticity, and to which even physics themselves must conform. Things of physics are after all things of actuality. Fundamentally this reduces to absurdity any creditworthy belief in the possibility of spiritless human individuals being anything, or having any actuality of meaningful description at all. To constitute a truth and a reality beyond any final closing of eyes, an intelligible and uninterrupted durable entity is *necessary*. This is what we think of as the *true being*.

Life and experience in the world is a gift but its validation as a *truth*, or any form of reality, (and consequently endless), is underwritten solely by the constant inner voice of companionship that is mental and intelligible *being*. All human individuals are primarily *beings* that *also* exist.

Being While Existing

What can be 'hit with a hammer' is merely a *portion* of what is intelligible to us, and is therefore a *portion* only of all things real.

This leads to the inference that it is untrue and absurd that things only of the senses, like health or wealth, alone define what it is to experience human lives.

Such things are *portions* only of what is intelligible.

All beings of human kind are to be respected.

That said it is their cumulative private resolve by inquiry into what is intelligible, and their disposition of will, that determines their quality of life experience. The less contemplative a mindset, the more mechanistic, less ordered, and inevitably less meaningful is the life experience to be.

It is in this that any essential inequality lies.

Contents

CONTENTS 7

PREFACE... 9

PROLOGUE.. 11

THE PRIVATE AND THE COLLECTIVE 21

CHAPTER 1 – TRUTH AND APPEARANCE..21
CHAPTER 2 – POLITICAL WIT...33

FORMS AND TRUE REALITY 43

CHAPTER 3 – BODIES AND SHADOWS..43
CHAPTER 4 – NEITHER HERE NOR THERE, BUT BOTH......................61
CHAPTER 5 – REAL HERE AND REAL THERE......................................73

AN UNCHANGEABLE REALITY 85

CHAPTER 6 – INTELLIGIBILITY AND TRUTH....................................85
CHAPTER 7 – BINDING THE SENSIBLE WITH THE INTELLIGIBLE 103
CHAPTER 8 – MOTION AND REST 117
CHAPTER 9 – THE FORCED ISSUE OF METAPHYSICS 131
CHAPTER 10 – MAN AS IMMATERIAL ENTITY 147

EPILOGUE.. 163

APPENDICIES... 173

APPENDIX ONE – MAKING LINKS 173
APPENDIX TWO – LAWRENCE KOHLBERG....................................178
APPENDIX THREE – CONVERGENCE...181

RECOMMENDED FURTHER READING...................................... 197

AUTHORS TESTAMENT 198

PREFACE

The question that may well be raised by a pragmatist or a Charles Peirce to such a work as this, may well be along the lines that if its substance is to be believed, what difference may then be *actually* discerned, to an individuals experience of life? This is answered in the following way; uncertainty of private significance is removed; uncertainty as to any enduring meaning in personhood is erased, and a sense of an unseen, but abiding, reality, (to which we are all obliged to be a part), is reinforced and underwritten. This eradicates all fear of death and the sense of the loss of loved ones that otherwise death alleges. *There is no greater spirit of liberty than this.*

The core *oeuvre* of this book is the necessity of the metaphysic principle to problem solving and life resolution. Though it relies much on received themes of precedent, it is by synthesis of these and more, and in a topological way, that originality may be found. It is done in the cause of aiding individuals by making the right connections, between what can be felt within, and what can be known, so to clarify the terms of life and existence in our physics driven world.

It is aided by making the relevant connections between philosophers throughout time, and is indebted in particular to the known positions of Parmenides, Plato, Zeno, and, in general, to so many others who, by means of philosophy, have shared the thrill of Moses on encountering a promised land. Voyaging beyond the plains of living and experiencing, its intention is to lift the spirit of awareness of readers to a threshold of apprehending a *realityscape* where death is refused entry by its *insufficiency* to meet the necessary requirements of *truth*.

Apprehension of such knowledge by the means adopted in this work, is proscribed by Bertrand Russell, claiming that *facts*, (if defined as rigid features of *knowledge* always endowed with actuality, truth, and reality), are discovered 'by observation and not by reasoning', but this is abundantly clear not to be the case.

Truth, or reality, (or features of this we can *know* as *facts*, as we shall see), often rely on things *unobservable*, while, at the same time, subsequent to rumination, often they are confirmed. We need only to think of Leonardo's drawings of tanks and submarines here. Unobservable in his time, even then they were potential, if not generally recognised or *known as facts*, and were clearly always fragments of truth and reality. *Facts*, (things *known to be*, even if they don't *exist*), are simply not required to be captured in what is instanced or phenomenalised. Any *theory* will rely upon *supposed* 'facts', (making it a 'theory'), and it is only the *grounds for such supposition* that requires appraisal and can make such facts actual, observable or not.

The work aims to show that any list of names of the dead on a stone tablet is an intelligible description of changes in time *of* meaningful things; a description of progress of things through motion, space and time. This is a description of a procedure of physics. What it is not is a description of things-in-themselves, undergoing that procedure of change in physics. *What is true and real, and rites of passage through physics, are distinct and different things.*

This is the complete meaning of what Parmenides claims so long ago, so often smoothly dismissed since as no more than a play on mere language. In fact he intends to make clear that anything we are justified to state *is* has unchangeable and ongoing qualification as a thing with *truth of being.* This condition or truth of being is entirely distinct from anything of finite nature, and even any finite properties as they may apply to some given object of contemplation. This object must be *intelligible* whether it is manifest or not as any tactile phenomenon.

It is intelligibility connects beings of truth with any finite properties with which they may be *also* associated, but it is only their origination in truth that authenticates both a thing-in-itself *and* any attributes it may claim, (within physics or beyond), rendering them meaningful, and cognisant always thereafter, (either in any measure of time that physics offers, *or* beyond). This thread of intelligibility and unalterable truth orchestrates the harmony we recognise as the *logos*, or vast order of intelligibility. As I have imaged this elsewhere, truth, (the order of logos), is like the infinite rope in the length of which there are an infinite number of knots, (events, human individuals, and separate things of identity). It is the rope, (truth) of which all the individual and separate things are composed.

Such perspicuity as this book may possess in easing the recognition of these things, is due in no meagre measure to the astute editorial contribution made by Timothy. I am confident that in consequence of his input, all that remains due from any reader is a responsive and sensitised inner and private mind's eye, offering access to encouraging, and life enhancing truths, that I have myself by giants been aided to apprehend. My hope and expectation therefore, is that it can only offer benefit.

PROLOGUE

There is no independent reality to physics or material bodies.

The observable world is composed of myself, others resembling me, and many classes of things that differ from both. The extent of the observable world at this period of time actually includes the universe due to advances in technology, but the extent of all that can be, including these things, is unmeasurable, though *some* total extent of *all* that can ever be is difficult to refute. We can have no idea of such an ultimate total of all things that can ever be, as a collection of *all* things of truth, yet without understanding what it may compass, such a total of everything is a plausible expectation. Without this notion pursuit of theoretical physics lacks drive or incentive.

As we approach grasping such an expectation, it is necessary to classify and distinguish things we consider true and real that can be *observed*, from those true and real that cannot. Things that *cannot* be observed are *ascertained*, (inferred and apprehended), by *mind*, as alternative to the eye. Our way of distinguishing them is by discerning there are 'things-in-themselves' to which we attribute physics, *as well as* the 'things-in-themselves' to which we attribute metaphysics.

Things that compose physics are finite and material things, episodic in time, and occupying space, while what composes metaphysics are abstractions, though objects of certain truth, that pertain always. While *human* confirms the variety of *life* of a member of a species, *being* confirms the *truth* of it. What is of truth is given as changeless and endless, and cannot become untrue. What lives must end. What is true cannot.

Plato's *world* of 'appearance', and *world* of intelligibility, can be misleading in that we normally associate 'world' with sensory things, but an appearance is required to be *of* something, and something of substantive truth, (this is his world of intelligibility), while making its appearance in physics, (or the sensory world). Any 'thing', (of either world), is a necessary fragment we may say, among many others that are necessary to compose the *whole of all true things*, much as Hegel would suggest.

The frame of metaphysics is sufficient to be composed of *all* true things, including physics, enabling both material and non-material things to be 'brothers in truth'. This bestows upon all things claimed to be real, including things of physics, an eternality or perpetuity, converging with the assertion of Parmenides that no true thing can ever 'cease to be'. This is required to be as true of an apple as much as it is of a man.

An implication of all this is that a human individual cannot be explained merely in terms of physics, and the material possession of a body. Existence of any finite dimension is a form within physics, but if *truly* this, also, then, simultaneously, it is necessarily an object of truth within metaphysics. This is what can be found to underwrite the immortality of man. All this is intelligible by the grace of *mind*, bridging life and existence with being of truth; physics and *material presence* entwined with metaphysics and *truth of being*.

In the case of Avicenna, it is demonstrated that by thought is a 'generality of forms' unveiled, distinguishing 'categories' and genera. It is not by what is manifest in physics that the origination of 'things' is determined, but by their derivation from the *metaphysic form* of a true and real *idea*. This makes of things of physics a short-lived *expression* of the metaphysic *being* of things aspiring to be truth. The buttercup for example is an expression of an an idea.

It is in the same way a house is simply *form* in the world of physics, an expression of thought and idea. The house being the truth always is unchangeable, regardless of any passage of time, and even when it is demolished. Truth dispenses perpetuity and eternality, whether within, or beyond, time.

Physics are deducible as truth *because* they are derived of a metaphysic *truth of being*. It follows that *substance* is ascertained more as an *essence*, a *being*, (an abstraction), than a physical thing within space and time. There is no thing of truth without its *being* that underwrites it under the metaphysic principle.

Unlike *objects of thing* perceived in the world of physics, like trees and houses, *objects of abstraction*, like justice and beauty, have no shape or colour etc that assemble into *form* of perceivable variety. This does not however render them *formless*, but on the contrary, renders *form of a different order*. They present form as *objects to thought* and are accessed by mind, and this we describe as *conceiving*, in direct contrast to *perceiving*, through the senses, *objects of thing*. We are all obliged to engage with conceiving *as well as* perceiving. This distinction of opposing forms, demanding attention for properly orientated experience of living, is a reduction to absurdity of the materialists claim that there is nothing real *except* matter.

When unadulterated justice or beauty are fully engaged, they cannot be falsehood and can only be truth. Such abstraction as objects to thought may be said to have true *being*. They are not required to be *in any given place nor in any given time*, but as fragments of any whole truth, (which I come to later), always they are accessible to 'mind'. This typifies the force and strength of meaningful and true things that have uninterrupted being as metaphysic form, (things beyond physics). Always they are truth and *cannot* be false. The same cannot be claimed of objects of thing relying as they must on time and place, for what appears to be a form of a ship on a distant horizon may well turn out to be true *or* false, depending on whether it may be illusory.

There are those, like the materialist, that engage with the world as if it were their duty to compound the miseries of their fellows, failing to understand that in so doing they compound their own also. Without sufficient wit or predilection to engage with ultimate truth and justice, such men are face to face with 'restlessness built into everything short of death', and never achieve a wholesome inner peace. Ignorance of the natural bounty of the world and our fellows, attainable by a well directed while enquiring life experience, lures such men to distance themselves from reality, and from each other, so reducing them to mere spectres 'who sleep in unvisited graves'.

However it may critically be defamed, the springboard and philosophic attitude of this series is grounded in both *intellective* and *emotional* love. This theme is the received object of wisdom in the work of artists, poets, and philosophers as threshold for inquiry and introspection, contemplated as a dependable indicator of truth and reality at one with the metaphysic principle.

All efforts made to debase this principle are doomed to failure, as all abstract entities are themselves meaningful to sensible life experience, and are pillars asserting the principle's commanding authority. None of these abstractions rest with physics, but lie beyond them, which is what is meant by metaphysics. Whether we contemplate 'universals', like goodness or whiteness, 'number', with its perpetuity, 'thought objects', like intellective or emotional love, the metaphysic principle applies. As for the significance of love, of either variety, or in combination, we have it again in the abstractions employed by practices of psychology that inform both human *life* and *being*. Whatever we may *love* is always as much an object of thought as it is an object of thing, whether we encounter it in what we *feel* or what we *see*.

Love at its greatest intensity is found in the human family, where rivalries, grief, and even hatreds often intrude in the service of daemons. All such interlopers are forms of negation to love, often carrying solicitous entry to real or imagined *pleasures* as they lead us away from the enduring *joy* of greater value that love per se supports. This is no less than tragedy on both private and familial scale, but can also spread its tentacles so far as to bring the disintegration of a whole society. Divorce, often encouraged and eased by hedonistic governance, is too ready an affidavit of love's broken promise and betrayal. It signifies only an insincerity of a faith and tryst made, or the weakness and fragility of a mindset unable to meet the personal sacrifice that love unerringly repays in abundant joy.

Intellective love applies greater focus, as paradigm, with human face *imagery*, looks, voice, signs of intent, and even *abstract objects* to thought, while emotive love may lay a greater, or even erotic, focus on 'bodies', words spoken, or things more tactile. Love may even bring both intellective and emotive appeal together in *one* object of contemplation. Intellective love carries the clear advantage in that it does not confine focus to the corporeal, (what is physical), as exemplified in love of God, love of truth, love of the dead, and so on, things little engaging with what arouses simultaneously sensual interest, or the erotic. This is love as object of thought and not of thing. Again the metaphysic principle will not be ignored.

Books of this series, the Philosophy of Feeling, and Durability and Truth, are concerned with self-authenticity, and self-resolution, evoking inner peace. This central theme is intended to promote confidence on a basis of submission to what may reasonably be ascertained as *truth*, in accord with what intuitively we all 'feel'. What we feel are *dependable* objects of cherishment and love are secure only when they are found doubtless and endless. Such 'objects' are, (in the vein of this work), party to a reality dimension that is both unending and reassuring, making them grounded in an intelligible base.

While we live we are condemned to experiencing something in order fully to rely on it. This is not the same way that things intelligible only to thought, beyond therefore the natural data of the sensible world, yet sufficient to supply meaning, are received as reliable. These we *cannot* experience, and instead, they are *envisaged.* Hence we distinguish 'things', (phenomena), from 'things thought', (noumena). It follows that our best way of distinguishing how we may come to have any grasp of either must *also* be distinguished; 'things' by *experience,* whether first or second account, (confirming their intelligible truth and required *existence),* and realizing 'things thought', (or even intuitively felt, like love), by our vision and *cognisance* of their intelligible truth and required *being.*

This work attempts to unveil from the best of philosophy, (too often at times obscured by language used), a truth dimension beyond the governance of space and time. Convergence with any theological theme, as well may be thought, is no contrivance, but, in a certain frame of mind, a natural and evolutionary result of any unfettered search for truth, *not* according to laws of physics, but abstracted from and *beyond them,* wholly and devotedly faithful in this case, to the metaphysic principle.

The complete *personhood and identity* of any human individual is unavoidably mythological and illusory, unless some sufficiently reasoned procedure of underwriting its truth and reality can be found, and *then* it can be believed. Then are we able to recognise *reality* in it. This is the chief object contemplated by this series, aided and supported in particular by the work of Gabriel Marcel, who asserts that to *life* must be added the *truth* of it, perpetual *being,* if ever life experience itself is to be recognised *in any sense* as whole and complete, significant, and hence intelligible.

Given this is so, no human individual considered significant and true, can become untrue or false, albeit that his *life* must end. Personhood cannot be made false or untrue *by* the ending of life and physical existence, when throughout it and after it, *being* of a given person remains and always abides. Once this fact is wholly appreciated, the clear inference made, as Parmenides enables, two millennia ago, is that albeit no man *lives* always, no man's true *being* ever can 'cease to be'.

The case for the true vitalism of man, by inference, is that this is *not* dependent on his physical *life,* in a world governed and controlled by physics, but must, on the contrary, rest on his true reality of *being,* making him an object of intelligibility which *always* must obtain. The clearly arguable implication of this is that *all* true things, past, present, or to come, (including the life experience of human individuals), as *necessary* fragments of any whole, complete, and unchangeable realityscape, must always abide, and cannot end or 'cease to be', however *time* brings either change or ending to the *existence* of physical things. Such change has no affect whatsoever on their *being of truth*, as distinct entities of abstraction. *Ending*, for abstract entity *being*, as a fragment of truth, is quite impossible. A number five cannot manifest itself in a field, stop being itself, or become something other. Always it is what it is.

Something emergent from close observational work in creative arts, particularly drawing and painting, and demonstrable in varying cultures and epochs of Art history, is the natural inclination towards readily recognised, particular forms of 'things', with scant attention paid to something *less* readily observed though it is *essential*; space. Romanesque sculpture relief crushes easily recognised forms together while excluding space altogether. The more naive artist may spend labour and industry on the minutely detailed tactile *form* of a 'thing', (as if complete in itself alone, and in isolation from all else), while completely unaware of the space, light, and other things upon which it depends and that give it life. Often events in life force reappraisal upon us.

Life and being obliges us to recognise the oftime baffling mystery that we must be 'two in one', (what we think and what we do), for they are not always the same, so that on daily basis, we live with an awareness of two worlds of engagement, one somehow imminent and *here*, and pragmatic, and frequently another is at some distant place, *there*, which our thoughts may visit, a supportive and theoretical input for how we conduct ourselves. Both command our attention, for both are integral to any well-directed personhood.

Both are required also to compose any clear construct of truth and reality, to which our personhood is a necessary fragment, and both are necessary to be meaningful; only participation in both worlds authenticates us as fragments of the whole of all that can ever be, authenticating us as at once a fragment of reality, while fully also *whole* in personhood.

We regularly explore this dual vitalism through the arts. It is necessary that we must *reconcile* inwardly with *both* worlds, for our life, *and* our being, (supportive of thought), are irreversible features of one singular and unending identity, like the 'sides of a coin'. Testimony of this lies in our ongoing love for those no longer about us or even living. Though we may die, nevertheless, we do not 'cease to *be*'. It is truth and reality, and not our body, which is the underwriter of this 'raw' *fact*, making what is *intelligible* of us, sufficient as something *greater* and more ongoing, than anything merely physical that individually we represent.

What typifies encounters with these two worlds, is engagement with what we recognise as 'things', and what we recognise as 'thoughts' of things. The one concerns physics and *life experience*, and is generally pragmatic and consequential, while the other concerns a *being of mind*, which is largely directive and instrumental, by means of will.

For balance and harmony, and unity, of personhood, both require well founded and reasoned, belief systems, inter-related, and sufficient to support clear intention, action, self worth, and direction. What is believed should not be based on superstition and private desires, or anything we are *told* to believe, but on what is sufficiently justifiable introspectively, so to sustain internalised relation, *between* what we think, and what we do. This is a *required* approach to self-authenticity.

We are aided in this by many works of philosophy, even in the case of those where wrong conclusions are drawn, which remain, nonetheless, priceless indicators of how justified and reasoned approaches may be grasped. I make the necessary connections between some of them, though not in an exhaustive way. I am quite sure further connections outside my focus here, are possible.

This for me has become a paradigm for how the sensible 'thing', (what we perceive with the senses), the thing in focus, tends to command primary attention, regarded as if it is the *sole* issue, the 'be all and end all', 'all that there is', and the sole true indicator, of any real and significant 'thing'. Yet no *sensible* delineation of it is possible at all without what is *unseen*, space at its boundaries, light, delineation from where other things 'begin', etc. Human lives are often perceived through the same restrictive veil. It is rather like when an object is focused against its supporting background through a camera lens, and what is supporting the meaning or significance of the object *in* focus is what is *not* in focus.

Given all this, and what we say and do are the *required* reality with which we must engage, (mediated by the thirdness of intelligibility, which is not going away anywhere), and, furthermore, that as truth, we never ourselves 'cease to be', except as living things, then our composition clearly cannot be alone of physics, time and space, (what we may call the life journey). We, and consequences we implement, are intelligible *and* unchangeable. Even in life, we are already beyond any rudimentary life plane, (as a twofold complex), in that our imperishable and unchanging *being*, (party to the intelligible principle informing *all* true things, the 'logos'), cannot, ever, be erased.

Human 'being', and quite unlike human 'living', is indifferent and wholly independent of, and contemptuous, of time. *Without* time all true things are obliged to *abide*, though they do not have to *exist* or live. What we think and do leads to self worth, or self rebuke, only by the ethereal and supersensory procedure of *what* we are thinking. Objects of thought have themselves no physicality, and so they cannot be grounded by time, the measure only of finite things. What is said and done leads to material outcome, which is in passing time, while the associated and related thought, *beyond* constraints of physics, and time, abides unchanged forever.' No great tragedy or joy is made greater or less by the passage of time'.

Time is an insufficient force to change the unchangeable, or the precise 'being' of anything. Propelled in *motion* through a world of physics, emotively and intellectively, we are at *rest* only in the 'blessed calm' of the unchanging world of contemplation. It is as if on the one hand, the world of the intelligible is something simultaneously aside and apart from the world of space and time, that our bodies inhabit for a while, while on the other, informing and substantiating them, and *all* that is true and real, so that we are simply not required to exclude *anything*, even from the true *significance* of physical things, (*because* of their core intelligibility), as does Plato, when clearly they *too* share it. Acceptance of noumenal truth and reality does not require the denial of it in phenomena, or the reduction of the latter to the Platonic notion of mere *representations*.

The contemplative world is the world of thirdness, and intelligibility. To explain what I mean by this it is necessary for a moment to diverge to the work of Charles Peirce to grasp the significance of the sort of *thirdness* to which I refer here.

Peirce adequately describes such a 'thirdness', when introducing us to his incisive and eloquent explanation of 'firstness', (our encounter of what presents to us), leading to 'secondness', (an interpretation of all connections or relations of such things to *other* things), and, importantly for us here, implying a supportive *thread* to which all of this inevitably leads us again, *thirdness*, which is *intelligibility*. We can envisage this as the 'glue' that *mediates* throughout firstness and secondness *and* holds all together, and hence is apprehendable as the necessary thirdness, not unlike the logos. This is something much greater a contribution to understanding than the pragmatism to which otherwise he seems generally devoted.

Firstness occurs whenever we encounter an *object*, be it one of physical presence, *or* one of thought and contemplation, its significance as a *complex*, dependent as it is on what constitutes its boundaries, and its relations to other things; its particular mass in a given space-time, if physical, or in the case of an idea, what constitutes all of it as against what does not. This is then the sign, (the semiotics of Peirce), *always*, for the same *class*, the same sort, of thing.

Secondness involves *interpretation* of the complex or a *developed* understanding. The *firstness*, he suggests, (the thing itself), spilling into *secondness* as it does, its relations with *other* things, (the developed understanding), an apple for example and its space, its attributes, or its distance from another object, is the full interpretation.

The idea 'beauty' also is a complex, a developed understanding, besides being a universal. The *mediator* informing us of it, (as well as endowing our apple), he rightly describes as *thirdness*, or intelligibility, (what grants distinctive and meaningful identity). Whether it is to be 'apple' or 'beauty', we have here actual *objects* of contemplation. It is so whether perceiving *or* conceiving. Never are they whole and complete in themselves, without their secondness, granting developed understanding, (all that they involve), which is intelligible, (mediated), and makes them intelligible to us. This is so whether we contemplate 'phenomena', or 'noumena'.

What is encountered clearly is beyond mere physical 'thingness'. What is intelligible, true, we are enabled *always* to contemplate *because* of its being so. Given all this, how, (unless devoted to material or pragmatic cause regardless), are we ever to claim that the notion of 'two worlds' composes merely a theory! How are human individuals to be regarded as no more than living beasts?

I am hopeful that within the limitations of a book of this sort, it will become possible, (for the reader who does not do so already), to see a man, a woman, a child, (as J.B. Priestley encourages), not merely as these 'things' alone, but *as* these, *'and something else'*, and that *this* is a perpetual and *intelligible entity*, which, timeless as it is, cannot be associated with only 'things' *past*, upon which clearly *memory*, (locked into the present dimension of time in physics), depends.

The private and the collective

Chapter 1 – Truth and Appearance

Rebellion confirms objection while revolution is a change of mind.
Without order, private mind is vulnerable to chance.
Order in things of motion, the finite, is derived best from eternal things at rest.

At many a turn in our lives, often we must revisit the terms of them, which is certainly the way to make some thematic sense and coherence of how it is that we come to say and do all that we do, and to feel utterly convinced, about where we should come to rest. This is the private and introspective way in which we find a method, either of bonding or breaking, with our time and place, where nothing is at rest, while simultaneously we encounter an alterity, or *otherness*, where things at rest are ubiquitous. A flower must indeed fade while its impact may not.

Affection, love, and triangles, are similar in that they neither are 'things' on trees nor are they 'things' in fields, and they have no solidity in space or time. Nonetheless, we know they are very true and real 'things' of some quite *different* order to solid things. Also we can understand from experience that *their* truth and reality obtains *always*, however any solid things, with which they may be associated, cannot do likewise. This different order to solid things connects with minds sensitised to it, for it is underwritten by intelligence; itself intelligible as an order, it is to 'mind' also intelligible.

The only reasonable inference to be made from this is that affection, love, triangles, and the like, have an ongoingness and durability, an 'unchangeability' which underpins a category or class of 'things' which never degenerate or go anywhere, but apply eternally as unassailable truths, constituting in their totality, a zone of reality. By its abstract nature, this zone admits thought and minds, but nothing physical. There is no such zone within space-time and physics, where change is unavoidable, which is why we attribute to rigid and changeless truths, where nothing changes, the nomenclature of *metaphysics*, in order to distinguish them as *beyond* physics.

Communication in sensory *life*, and within physical boundaries, of universal affection or love relies upon sufficient private interest within us, to engage with it, (as an element of our mental life), and a degree of shared empathy for the sentiment itself. Some live, as it were, in a fishbowl, devoid of such private interest, and although there is a whole reality beyond the bowl, in metaphysical terms, they may be so self- absorbed, or otherwise engaged, as not ever to see beyond the bowl.

This is where unreciprocated love or affection resides, in the bowl, often separating us, like the barrier of glass between where we are, and 'what we may be', so that only what 'seems' commands our attention, often instead of what is real and true. Love rejected is not love erased. To convey any enlightenment on sentiment to those sufficiently content to remain within such a metaphorical bowl, is to as much purpose as speaking German to a Chinese with no knowledge of it, so that neither words nor substance have meaning to him.

One avenue of escape from this lies in our affection for our fellows, and mutual esteem heightens our self worth, nourishing any resolve to conduct our lives to the benefit of the wider community, where it is then collectively cherished. It is now over half a century ago, that something of this kind, which began small, as an aesthetic energy peak, in a city or two, (Liverpool and almost simultaneously London), gained strength and unity of purpose.

Even across the Atlantic there was convergence in New York, with the aid of Alan Ginsberg, and from very localised inception, all this grew into a worldwide phenomenon; a cultural *rebellion* which developed into a cultural *revolution*, moving society universally, from a point of excessive conformity, and codes of impersonal principle, to an emphasis instead on the liberty of self expression, something so unconventional at the time as to be viewed as vulgar.

Reluctance to speak out, the convention, was dismantled. Of course, those taking this to excess, are now so industrious at it, sometimes to the exclusion of either insight or careful thought, that what they come up with is often more sonorous, or bogged in sensation, than meaningful. As can so often happen within any society, many today, whether artist or politician, seem to have 'lost the plot' of the founders of the cultural upheaval of half a century ago, and are more guided by self-acclaim than significance.

It is to our collective discredit that this movement has been 'hijacked' by the vulgar themselves, who have translated it into a 'free for all' and opportunist sentiment for all individuals to do and say as they like, which leads to the opposite intention to its founders, so that love and care of our fellows and our own self worth has been 'traded in' for egoism, hedonism, and too frequent social abuse.

This has permeated the whole of present society, so that it is built into the politick of the establishment, leaving us again confronted by the need of another, and formidable, thoughtful *rebellion* if there is to be any hope of overcoming the confused thinking which informs it. The happy combination dispensed by nature to human *being,* self worth *and* humility, requires renaissance. Once reluctant to speak out, the new convention is vocal incontinence, where *anything* is permissible. If we are to be hopeful of improvement, this must be overthrown.

Any brief period of social history has no more relevance than that of an episode of time, and the larger issues grasped by this thesis are far greater than even time itself. It is clear that private resolution *can,* ultimately, generate collective reappraisal. This gives us all hope, that by some cultural rebellion, a sense of fellowship, and value can be renewed, so to face problems of 'why we are here', breaking repressive conventions. Today we have excessive rigour where it is absurd, and laxity conducive to spiritual poverty. Thus, repression is *not* erased, but replaced, and assumes a different guise, so that those individuals now most at risk are the young and the old. Aspirations such as independent thought and expression are often propagandised as villainous, bearing labels such as *sexist* and *racialist,* even where they are not.

What *now* is solely apparent of this vibrant neo 'Left Bank' culture, driven at first by Adrian Henri and associated artists, may be compared to the dark side of the moon, little apparent to us, obscure as merely a *fragment* which is something hidden. We convert what is hidden to what we perceive of it.

What took place for the collective unconscious of this land, was, and *is,* infinitely more consequential, than merely that of a time of reinvention for the pop music scene. We have a culture today preoccupied with appearance while hardly engaging at all with truth. This is left to chance discovery. Truth is deeper than what is readily found.

The deeper cultural rebellion, of which popular music was merely a symptom, was the linking of hands in fellowship for the value of individuation, badly needed at the time, but which now, and somewhat internationally, as it is grown, to revolutionary proportion, (though sadly, sometimes applied excessively for best consequence), represents a courageous step in closer self scrutiny aimed at the recognition of self worth in the sometime bewildering state of being human. The degree to which this is perverted and misconstrued is well represented periodically in the Turner Prize for celebrated 'artists', displaying little art. Better it should be named the 'Turner Prize for Celebrities'.

We must first acknowledge in our search for self worth, that this alone can be daunting enough, and that there is something greater still than ourselves, and that this too requires recognition. Although we have, as Schopenhauer suggests, a great power in the form of our will, it is clearly not this which gives us life, nor this which sustains us, and neither does it give us unlimited control over events. In spite of the admirable power of self-will then, true authorship of *all* things is not there, but elsewhere. Without this humbling antidote of awareness, tools at the disposal of the will are no more than shallow adornment in the misdirecting hands of leading 'celebrities'. This is no more than style without substance. Today, truth and greater awareness is again more needed, above appearances, just as it was half a century ago.

So self evident is the notion of cherishing what is not always the most obvious, that even the materialist ultimately is obliged to conciliate with it, though, habitually he clings stubbornly by the fingernails only to procedures relying on sense data that he purports to be the most reliable or correct route to solutions, in turn locking himself into expectations bounded by a sensory perimeter only. He is not at liberty and disqualifies himself from exploring what he regards disdainfully as metaphysical nonsense. He is content to allow neurophysics, though not an exact science itself, to attempt to explain things that he himself cannot, for this at least allows him to be loyal to his cause. For him, it is 'true and real' only by procedures of physics, which justify this, so it can be bottled with detailed precision.

What he loses by this is of no concern to him because, for him, without such private interest, predilectively, it must be excluded anyway. He has no such intuitive insight, sense, or feeling. Certain of the Liverpool rebels half a century ago did *not* so confine themselves, as in the cases of Adrian Henri, Sam Walsh, Stuart Sutcliffe and the like, but were prepared, audaciously, and necessarily in non-conformist ways, to 'rush where angels feared to tread', and even in the teeth of criticism, and it was *this* they brushed aside with conviction.

It was not some initiative confined to musicians alone, who were themselves inspired by the dynamic of the practicing artists. The primary incentive of the Beatles or Merseysippi Jazz Band was a *contribution* to the cultural ethos of rebelliousness in time and place. The so-called Liverpool Scene *included* musicians, and was not *their* invention alone, (the phrase actually *coined* by Adrian Henri), though this is a reversal of the received wisdom. While a rebellion drew attention through popular music, the revolution growing from artists work less conspicuously continued its infiltration exponentially, lastingly changing society as a whole more profoundly.

Often the upheaval, engendered at the time, derived from little more than what artists could express as a *feeling*, which informed their work. However insubstantial the life and work of Christ, to many, the love for it of Arthur Dooley sprang in excess of twenty feet high, in his tortuous expression of the crucifixion incorporating barbed wire and torn rag. This he lodged as a very large wedding present with Rod Murray, an artist of notable and quite different iconic works, for safekeeping.

Dooley brought to his work the immediate appeal of coarse materials, with which he was so familiar from his days as a docker and labourer, and ultimately he was to leave his mark, (like that of mediaeval workers), in churches to the north. The recognition of his self worth, with his humble beginnings, by his fellow artists and the public in the north of this land, repeatedly astonished him, while nourishing his sense of self worth. He had found himself with a life of both *substance* as well as style.

When, intellectively, and intuitively, we sense something *unseen*, as such an artist must, feeling sure it is 'accessible', (however seemingly private in appeal), it is the duty of our tactile senses to question it, and even to tell us that we are trying to understand something which, (as yet anyway), truly is 'not really there' until the occasion when it is materialised by a sculptor; until then it is merely something only of which we *think*, for there is no 'thing' solid and identical to what is envisaged by thought, already in the world.

A well-driven artist however is at liberty to make it *appear* in the world. He makes it in fact *exist*. Those willingly confining themselves generally only to what is *sensory*, pragmatic, or to 'sensible' things, (things bearing sense data), may even ridicule what they regard as futile labour, which can often account for the low esteem in which the artist's innovations are regarded. The magic his craft enables him to perform has made something move from what is unseen to what is seen, and he has *bridged* two worlds, however many may ignore this.

The course of the materialist is quite an insufficient course to artists of style *and* substance, who by nature presuppose the truth and reality of things covering much broader spectrum than merely physical things, so to include *intelligible* if unseen things, some of which spring from a passionate intensity, ultimately reaching into the world of the senses.

Though only *one* may know the *substance* of a work performed at inception, touched by the potter's hand, it is placed in the physical world. Neither can the potter know all that is possible at the hand of others. Without recognition of this, improvement and advance in the human condition would be impossible. Empathy of assumed integrity between individuals must be presupposed, as was indeed the case with the cultural rebellion of half a century ago. No less than an alliance of poet, painter, musician and philosopher in common cause.

As the materialist must devise a way to allow this also, he constructs a *logic* of pragmatics, so that it is the needs of humans which dictate what is intelligible, as demonstrated in laws, ethics, and social needs, (not to mention the neurophysics on an individual level to which I refer above, and which for him originates *all* we say and do). Notions of cosmic order, intellective deliberation, a 'logos', a 'sigma', or something 'behind everything', and quite indifferent to humanly inspired and evaluated criteria, is *not* a consideration of his private interests. We may, however, take it as given, that humanity will not, individually *or* collectively, be consulted when our sun becomes a 'red giant', or the earth herself sterile.

The ready alternative offered by Hume that everything is a matter of 'random conjunction', upon which, in a fit of intellective neurosis, we superimpose patterns of our own, already was discredited, however many may choose to ignore this, by his own time. It may be observed in the drawings of Leonardo, the work of Brunelleschi, and much else beside. It is like the offer of a blindfold to those who wish to deny their sight. Full devotion to such a thing could have denied our stepping on the moon.

Pattern making is not the superimposition arbitrarily made across essentially random circumstances, but the discovery of intelligible relations and interrelations between particular things. It is the mediation between intelligible things as they become intelligible to us. There is an abundance of evidence to the contrary of 'random conjunction' from the first application of magnetic rock, through the drawings of master artists, to the advances of modern science and technology. Even by the time of Hume this should have been abundantly clear.

The mystery of a true and real triangle is that it does not grow in fields. We have no choice but to satisfy a yearning, which originated *within* us, to grasp at some 'handle' on things so the better to understand them. Uncovering 'patterns' is no more than a required approach to this, the mediating relation between what *is*, in truth, intelligible, and what is apprehendable *of it* by intelligent mental life. Such things have no *required* practicality, however they may result in practical outcome.

The *clock in the sky* is something of astronomic and very real significance we may consider a worthy candidate for the mere random Humean conjunction upon which we *overlay* a pattern of meaning. It is a calculable correlation between the 'plough' group of stars and Polaris, (the North Star), that is capable of giving us the correct time on earth, a precise and accurate geophysical feature of our very real place in space and time, or physics. This relation with its pattern is no invention.

The trouble is, if this is a random and unintentional accident, for there can be no meaningful or intelligible patterning in the order of the cosmos, how is it that there is, and further, how is it meaningful only to intelligent beings, and not absurd as a mere product of random and chance? Are we expected to believe that all patterns of meaning we discover are somehow fiction? Frankly, it is far easier to believe that such events are indeed fragments of great order in all things. Could penicillin ever have been discovered if it had not true being *before* it was intelligible to us? Surely our patterning and understanding follows only what truly *is*. How is it then to be false?

Some look to science generally, and stubbornly, for some monopolised 'handle' on things, but the business of science merely explores how something is as it is, and which clearly precedes its discovery of cipher or pattern. Some, desperate for *any* handle, however obscure or ill founded its origination, dispensing with personal responsibility and private decision-making, clutch at superstitions and religious cults.

Yet others, altogether happy or not, follow the various rationale of world faiths, which do, at least, carry, if no guarantee, the distinction greater than the religious cult, of plausibility, derived of some reasoning procedure that requires a patterning and order of relations. Such as these carry also, (rewarding a vibrant spirit), what we may think rhetorical questions; when we wish to offer gratitude, whom can we thank; when we are angry, to whom can we complain, and when we are sad and upset, who can comfort us? All such things are concerns of how we *feel* and meaningful to us.

For others there is even greater likelihood of emotional and intellective satisfaction by an astute topology, a reckoning and making of connections carrying the authenticity and credentials revealed by private introspective inquiry. This is not pattern *making*, but pattern-*discovery*. However or to whatever degree, solutions reached in this way, may be considered, or even castigated, as 'mystic', transcendent, or even revelatory, their private authenticity and private interest, self validates them, provided what we believe is well supported as *intelligible*, and there is good reason for the things to which we cling. As we shall see, there is reason for this.

For those who turn to politics, grasping at handles for understanding's sake is not what is contemplated, but rather is it a coquettish display of *knowing exactly* where men should go and how highest ideals are to be achieved. Arrogant zeal is its usual hallmark. Questioning anything in any profound way is dismissed in favour of pretended declaration of unknown things as if they were clear 'truths'.

Historically we live in yet another, (so oft are they repeated), period of over regulation and governance, where those who 'know better' see fit to drag furrows through the peace of our self-resolution. They make no distinction between things of private or public concern, and private liberty pays the price. Internationally, where men prefer *autocracy* for governance, this must, by force where necessary, be transformed into some variety of *democracy* that someone with sufficient power feels must be 'better', even though his understanding of *both* political animals is impoverished.

Indeed, leaders *know*, and apprehend *change* from what they have *mis*construed of our journey, though ill-equipped to distinguish whether we have all 'progressed' or 'regressed' since half a century before. The puzzle of it overtaxes them so, they focus on political industry that is energetic while absurd, and where force is applied, it is not only illegal, but also intemperate, and wholly objectionable. Their foreign policies leave the Middle East to the 'survival of the fittest' at the time of writing.

Nationally, private pursuits or habits, however innocuous, are outlawed by the majority, regardless of the views of minorities, for this is democratic, and we all know and accept, (it is assumed), that this is a *virtuous* politick. Such is the measure of wit of some varieties of democratic rule, in spite of the lessons of Ancient Greece. *Equality* is taken to such lengths, in such a variety of democracy, that, as Socrates foretold, over two thousand years ago, ordinary 'citizens will brush shoulders with criminals in the street'. Even in terms of education, excellence is inadmissible unless by statute we contrive an *appearance* of it in *everyone*, so that equality, the *prime* objective, is achieved, while marginalizing the outrageous anomaly of individual excellence. Excellence is not the object contemplated here, but *equality*.

If in fact uniform equality were to be a *real* truth-value, rather than the fictional ideal that it is, then there could be nothing to aspire to and no route to 'bettering oneself' or self-improvement. Nature would ensure that all men should be of equal size and strength, and individuation could severely be punished. Even nature does not seem to acknowledge such a standard criteria. As an ultimate achievement of such political misdirection all private hope or aspiration for self-betterment or improvement should be rendered redundant. Nowhere on earth could we encounter again an example of the 'noble savage'.

The ability to *distinguish and discriminate* what is good, what is bad, what is desirable or not, what is better than something else, and generally to perceive what may be wise or unwise, (and quite regardless of any acumen used in this process), is by language disenfranchised and paralysed. Such a procedure is devalued by a 'tsunamic wave' of excessive liberalism, condemning it, with propaganda designed for the purpose, so that those who persist in prudently applying 'discrimination' under *any* circumstances are declared mentally unfit, (phobic), 'judgemental', (an odious and clumsy word), or racialist, if not conforming with the *dogma* of popular liberalism, however confused or absurd may be, what widely *it* acclaims.

In downgrading perennial values, (which in truth should be based not on *ethics* but on *virtue*), Parliament would seem to come very close to fulfilling many of the expectations of the benevolent king with whom it warred and subsequently murdered, King Charles, and this, again, without justification or authority, other than its own. Then as now, it manufactures this to suit *any* occasion, (just as today it continues so to do), from the brute fact that for overcoming obstruction to its privy determinations, it requires only sufficient *power*. In some ways, the tyranny of yesterday is not unlike the tyranny today, both being negation of any benevolent order, where *all* may be expected to reach a position of rest, (harmony with ultimate justice). Such conduct is without any redeeming virtue, (*here* or *there*), and so, inevitably, must face ultimate self-defeat at the hands of wiser revision, a cause for hope for all.

Any form of governance, however it self extols virtue while inherently having it not, (mistakenly *presumed* from being 'democratic'), and prepared to ground itself on a basis of grave crime, as indeed *parliament* so did, in the case of King Charles, must remain open to question. Irrespective either of the lapse of passing time, or of its convenient amnesia in having appropriated the authority of the king, (it has made no attempt to express formal regret), it can hardly be described as an institution grounded in *virtue*. As it was a military coup, which installed the parliament we recognise today to begin with, ('amidst the clash of arms', says Cicero, 'the law is silent'), one is at liberty to question its moral legitimacy, and any statutory legislation since its inception. Rather is the parliament founded, (and not unlike the French Assembly), in murder, zeal, and covetousness, to the purpose of grasping power to itself, an appetite which even to this day would appear to be its first principle of choice.

Gone in this process with much else, is the recognition of benevolent influence from the king which was hundreds of years ahead of its time; institution of the first poor laws to show due consideration for the underprivileged; religious toleration in the face of ministerial opposition, and a patronage and encouragement for creativity through the liberal arts.

Clearly, and at any given time, we have models of order, both for individual minds and collectives, which are *earthbound*, often drawing the acclaim of shallow men who compose the restless and devoted processional wake for them into meaningless places. The alternative model of order, offering much more than this, cannot be encompassed by the earthbound things alone, and has no shortage of sober and tranquil guests.

In this context should we begin the chapter to follow by assessing how, in the view of such guests, the new politick benefits modern society, or even whether it can be seen so to do at all. This facilitates reaching my chief object contemplated in this work, namely how we must recognise the *true* from the *apparent* in any attempt to self revise, and resolve ourselves, (by discernment of what is durable and what is not), and I review the social and governmental notions prevailing at the beginning of the second millennia as witnessed in this land today, and as it applies to Western ideology.

Chapter 2 – Political Wit

Political theories are man's synthetic attempts to control his fall from virtue.
'An arrogant pretence of controlling events'.

Any government of people, past or present, which stifles, curbs, or manipulates, the voice of its people, making statute law forbidding or inhibiting views opposing its own, so excluding effective objection to its unmandate decisions, as with its agenda today to marginalise 'nationhood' and replace this with a synthetic 'statehood', is nothing short of iniquitous. Such governance implying public assent never sought, on a foundational issue, clearly without specified consent, and *imposed*, robs citizens who cherish their inheritance of a distinctive and natural identity from their forbears.

Compelled by law citizens are expected to embrace a *political* identity, or to have none at all, with racial 'law', forbidding any distinction between the needs of one citizen as against another, the means of *enforcement*. In the cause of some fictional, if even attainable, 'globalism' of culture, indigenous cultural identity is to be trashed. Possession of *power* to effect this is once again the key.

Tyranny evolves from such 'dictat' of those with power, who promise one thing to attain it, and do what they like once they have it, always having at their disposal the excuse that they must engage in privileged debate, however disingenuous or perverse, an institutionalised government may be inclined to make this, as so often in the case of 'party' politics. After all, the offer of 'party' to an electorate is the offer of a straightjacket mentality, a rigid dogmatism, and especially in the case of one that outlaws and disbands any likely or possible objection, from any impartial and objective arbiter, such as the House of Lords once was, and as for generations, it conducted itself.

While innocent human corpses may have accorded with law in the Third Reich, (statute law of its own invention), likewise is it the corpse of liberty, (whether of natural national identity, freedom of speech, right of private pursuits, etc.), that accords with law at the hands of parliament. What both systems of law share, is the *power* to have their way with us, and, in parliament's case today, objection to its collective view, under law, (arbitration by the House of Lords effectively neutered), is not to be tolerated, even to the extent that one may be prosecuted, under law, for the use of a word or words, even where it may include considering the prosecution of children for such unguardedness. Something particularly shared with the Third Reich.

Self-resolution, which is authentic and meaningful, is the 'cause' of my Philosophy Of Feeling series, of which this is the second book. Connections are readily recognised between our forbears and ourselves, and often the same mistakes are repeated, or, better than this, avoided. It would be a first step of advance if it were *required* of those who would be our leaders that first they study the classics, and had some profitable exposure in their education to events and ideas as they are astutely posited in history, and not either as they *imagine* them, or *desire* them, to be, something sadly lacking today in their foolish trampling through the political and cultural world.

In the cultural area the intrusion and manipulation for the political aim of serving equality to the extent of ironing out all things that do not conform to the ideology of the time, has had a debilitating affect on Art education at all levels. Although political ideologies should have no rightful place in such an area, *sameness* has been engineered throughout the art schools since conformity was first introduced in the 1960's within the United Kingdom.

The independent character with all the advantages this carries, of Art schools like Chelsea, Camberwell, and Wimbledon, are now swallowed into an administered and controlled singled unit. Amalgamation of this sort necessitates loss of identity in the cause of some hierarchical and uniform aim, which has more likelihood of being as damaging, as it may in some ways be beneficial, for administration purposes.

Though at one time schools were distinctive by their sculptural, graphic, or painting expertise, all are now generally submissive to political influence and received ideology. The distinctive flavours favoured by individual schools are now submerged into a common 'gruel' of widespread similarity. An equally shared standard of correctness is the result, even in tutoring and especially at secondary level of schooling, where 'teachers' trained by the 'machine' labour industriously at which particular experience of materials pupils should be exposed to while having little to offer as to what should be done with them. The politic of 'equality' self-validates anything original as valid, however inept, visually illiterate, or trivial.

This seems to endorse and reinforce, especially in the present populist and celebrity culture, the old tenet that a society produces the quality of art that reflects it. It is to be hoped that the rebellious distinctive 'artist in the garret' may yet offer hope of escape to a more meaningful future. In such a climate, popularity will not be served to him on a plate, but the heroic requires stubbornness and devotion in any worthy cause.

Progress is not something that applies to ourselves alone, bestowing some badge of honour on our sleeve, (so to enhance our standing against our forbears), but an efficacy measure of our procedures in applying ourselves to problems the world poses, and with which we wish to engage. Such an understanding leads us to a respect for our forbears in the past, even to take instruction from them.

Similarly, when philosophy reduces politics to 'an arrogant pretence of controlling events', it serves well to highlight the ignorance and arrogance of those who traffic ready solutions to all men by sundry incompetent politick. 'All men *must* be democrats' is just such a solution. Equally, when it comes to political thinking, it is a problem. Likewise, the true artist is licensed to withstand the onslaught of triviality that seeks to diminish the oeuvre of the genuine artist. The very word itself is trivialised appended to all and sundry, even pop musicians, so that it carries no association with excellence, only with relevance, to a society worshipping sensation. The same priority squeezes out notions of morality. A dominant culture of inane wit reigns.

William of Ockham's preference for the parallel authority appropriate to both church and state, where indeed they may be of counsellory benefit to each other on matters of difficulty, (spiritual and temporal), has never truly yet been implemented. Today, each would seem to receive the other's counsel as unwanted interference. Neither did he dismiss *autocracy* as a form of governance, as in his view it is the undeniable right of the populace to remove inept rulers, of whatever status. There is much in the views of Thomas Hobbes that may be argued as convergent. If there is fault, it is in those who define politics as maximising all that is inherently good in democracy *alone*. It was indeed a variety of democracy that led to the precipitant death of one of our greatest mentors of humanity, Socrates, on account of his opposition to it.

There are many varieties of democracy to which politicians may aspire, though rarely do they seem today to be aware of this. There is *formal* democracy, (the most authoritarian), *informal* democracy, (the most fluent), and *liberal* democracy, (the most inept), to name the most obvious. Informal democracy carries with it a spirit of liberty which permeates its political ideology, and thus offers citizenry genuine choices of ongoing relevance to events. Senatorial governance is a paradigm means of effecting this.

A senate allows, (unlike Parliament today), greater opportunity for the fulfilment of *general will*, (in the Rousseau way), delivering the effective cherishment of private liberty allied to an *order* of republican character. Under the guardianship of such a state I obey laws, as a citizen, that arise from my own private will, interests, and desires. It is not *parties*, with dogmatic agendas of ideological and academic substance that have nothing to do with my private interests that then govern me, but *senators* who transmit my interests to the central governing power that enforces them, with regard always for the private sense of liberty that I cherish. Parliament has no such purpose.

Formal democracy cannot do this, imposing dogmatic legislation not by mandate designed to offer to citizenry opportunity to authorise it, but, instead, designed to gain power, and occasionally squeezing out of such commitments as they may have made before gaining it. Periods of election and acquiescence from the citizenry, anyway, are so widely set apart in time that cleverly it finds itself with unimpeded liberty, in the intervals, to do as it will. This gives it opportunity to go to war *without* the consent of citizens, or, according to its own agendas, even institute laws that intrude into those very citizens' private lives who elected it, (which is none of its business).

It is for this reason that, with the best of intention recognised, I believe Karl Popper's preferred 'liberal democracy' to be an error of definition. It carries built in propensity for widespread laxity, such as Socrates describes, allowing citizens to do as they like without sanction, where, as related above, 'even the criminals brush shoulders with the ordinary citizen in the street', and even to abandon common sense. This is just as extreme as are the contrary excesses of governance found in Formal democracy. For the vulgar however, it is a popular and hopelessly inept notion of *freedom.*

It is clear that while Formal democracy is unnecessarily tight and rigid, (benefiting governors more than the governed), Liberal democracy, on the contrary, encourages excessive laxity, which can be so extreme as to lead to social disintegration. This is no more to be preferred to Formal democracy, where citizenry are permitted only at wide intervals of several years either to have any input into important legislation, or to change their leadership. This approaches a closed system allowing foolish leadership unbridled freedom for just as long.

Paradigm foolishness, (and courtship with future problems), can readily be recognised in the inept solution frequently emphasised by today's formal and authoritarian variety of democracy, to ignore our ancestors, our tribal origin, our provenance, or any cultural legacy to which we are due, indeed, to pretend none of us have one, superimposing an amorphous *political* category over *all* citizens. This is *statehood* of which we must speak, and with which we must engage, over and above any true and real nature of *nationhood* we inherit from our forbears. Statehood, or more precisely, *nationality*, is a political classification, and is *transferable*. *Nationhood* is a genetic and anthropological classification, and *unalterable*.

Confusing the two imitates the political paradigm of the fledgling United States, where if any social cohesion is to seen at all, this can only be done in terms of the political and synthetic. Any resulting cohesion is, also, therefore, entirely superficial *by* being political, for it *is* synthetic and contrived. Of course by its lack of meaning, privately and collectively, it sows also seeds of fractious discontent and dissention.

Denial of gender, (the clear fiction of 'unisex'), and denial of race, whether that of others or ourselves, is a refusal to accept what *is*, (the clear truth), or the status of something with which we are face-to-face. This negates self-meaning and authenticity. It deprives individuals of birthright. To *politicise* such things in the cause of overlaying an *absolute of equality*, is to add insult to injury. This is when it is most iniquitous as propaganda designed to engineer falsehood to replace the nature of nationhood with the synthetic of statehood, or sexuality with some indiscriminate androgyny. The latter fosters random and purposeless sexual expression at the cost of expelling *meaning* bearing *any* relation to truth.

Such politic, inevitably self-destructive and disordered, disintegrates social collective, normally reliant on a composition of hard-earned authentic and shared heritage of mature aspiration. This happens in the outright dismissal of nationhood for statehood, and is even demeaning for newcomers to a land, encouraged, as they are by this, to dismiss their provenance. It is a recipe for unhappiness and despair.

While men may live in a state, they do not live because of it.
It is their nation gives them life itself.

Terminology is so loosely engaged, and so ill conceived today as to become wholly meaningless. While it is true that an individual from anywhere in the world, a consequence of empire building, may legitimately be described as British, (a political term, as used in ancient Rome whether for Negroid or Celt), given he has just claim to the same, this does not mean, even if born in Wales or Scotland, that this is sufficient to make him also a Welshman or a Scot, (a nationhood term). Nationhood is not something open to ill-informed *vagaries* of *political* definition, but an ontological and anthropological brute fact. Of course laws that imply racial hatred, where nothing of the sort is intended, effectively proscribe such a truth being posited, though it is merely a statement of fact.

By such a course, we disenfranchise and abuse the legacy and identity of both black *and* indigenous cultures, encouraging them to adopt an amnesiac and totally political, (and disinherited), identity, trammelled by the ill informed, and which is the result of manipulation. Triumphantly declaring the virtue of this *synthetic identity* applicable by political manoeuvre to all, the self-contradictory and propagandist terminology of a so-called 'multiculture', (demonstrable only in some idealist and fanciful world where nationhood is meaningless), and its inventive doctrine, replaces meaning and self worth.

In such a melee of disorder, terrorism is the wholly unacceptable, yet predictable, resort of resistance for those suffering the loss of their meaning. What is at once 'many' cannot be claimed, simultaneously, to be some *singular* culture. Advancing by infant steps, political gurus now wish to favour 'integration' as the ultimate answer to the dysfunctional 'multiculture' that they themselves engineered. Finding difficulty with their first approach, they turn to compounding their confused thinking, and their failure to distinguish between nationhood and statehood. Such nonsense, privately or collectively, courts only tears.

Our identity and cultural heritage, true, real, and important to us, (whether by genetic or sentiment recognition), can only be ignored at private and public peril, yet is irresponsibly waived to be replaced by the impermanent, floating, and vacuous political doctrine favoured by arrogant and ill-informed leaders devoted to idiosyncratic idealism, and, as indicated above, implemented by their possession of sufficient *power*. They have not sufficient wit to realise that Nationalist sentiment grants dignity and identity to *all* peoples, and not, as they imagine, to any one particular people *over* others.

Our present variety of liberal democracy denies the truth of this to enhance itself. The object they reflexively contemplate is *not* truth, or reality, but political engineering to achieve their unchallenged authority. The adoption of the populist misconception that Nationalism represents nothing other than totalitarianism, and to build the state, *on* this misconception, at best, (and falsehood at worst), in order to disenchant the very notion of Nationalism, instead of delivering justice and liberty for all by wiser means, is irresponsible.

Concurrent and in addition to their confused thinking, they institute law to support it, not in relation to the virtues, (but by ethical dictat), and this is clearly just as St Augustine suggests, providing government no better than a 'band of robbers'. The citizenry is robbed of wise governance, leaving the indigenous confused, and the immigrant with no clear identity of anything with which to engage, in what for him already is a challenge, that he must face with courage, of new life, away *from* the legacy and culture and 'heimat' of his own forbears. Indeed, where he feels he perceives a cultural vacuum, it is natural he should feel the need to inject his own. For the host nation this is at the least irritating.

We are, however, favoured by the view of Socrates in that from generation to generation, men often display the consistency and true grasp of things of grasshoppers. In this book, and by visiting truth and reality, it is our business to find what does *not* change in such a capricious way, as *political* thought is so apt to do, subject as it is to manacled dogma. Our liberty of thought, expression, and action, whether privately or publicly, must be defended against inept law, not by militant rebellion, but, as Karl Popper may put it, 'peacefully and regularly' changing our leaders, which formal democracy frowns upon, fearing incursion into its power, so that it offers only limited revision of its 'periods of domination', at times so prolonged, as to be potentially dangerous.

This is not an option offering clear and unobstructed voice at the level of nation management. Cromwell's Parliament is obsolete, archaic, and the autocratic and dictatorial martial product of a martial mind, his own. Its accountability self orientates like some supernatural oracle. Rather than a system of capricious representation by unreliable and self-opinionated members, often placing self interest, or party interest, first, often following the dictate of some leading fool, the world would do well to imitate, (from practical necessity of preferring *some* form of governance rather than *none*), the classic *senatorial system*. Members of this, of course, are appointed *specifically*, (according to tradition), to give the voice required by the citizenry at large, and, as more likely, comprehensively, without 'exclusion clauses' from public criticism, such as the proverbial 'having to listen to debate'.

It is true that politics must, in the more liberal sense, resolve issues by means of negotiation and compromise, but as Professor Bellamy reminds, whilst 'compromise is a political virtue', it can hardly be regarded as a philosophical one. What is generally more applicable in what I say above, is the attitude of John Stuart Mill, who declared that it was 'unnecessary to consult' with his constituents, since he 'undoubtedly' knew their own best interests 'better than they themselves'. This arrogance is the received wisdom and daily manifesto of Cromwell's Parliament, and perhaps the natural consequence of wresting power and authority they themselves now appropriate with a property of *kingship* more excessive than that of the legitimate king they expunged. The new order, though now quite old, is live and well. What supports the 'throne' is power.

Politics show themselves willing historically to usurp the *authority* of philosophy when convenient to its own agenda, (as Plato, Voltaire, Heidegger, Sartre's, and many others experience), but always equally they show themselves impervious to its *wisdom*. When democracy is by received wisdom misconstrued as generally reading *virtue*, clearly nothing beneficial has been absorbed or fully appraised of the teaching and experience of Socrates. I am persuaded this is largely due to the prior aspiration of politics to gain and maintain *power and control*.

For the purposes of my thesis here, grounded in what does *not* change, politics have no useful input unless that be to effect aspirations from which only *true and real values* emerge, namely the universal, (some would say divinely inspired), and long established *virtues*. Present preoccupations with hedonistic self-gratification make that unlikely, for not only is spiritual worth ignored, but also by muddle-headedness and secular meddling, is true virtue, (by which humanity is enriched), obstructed, and supplanted by 'noticeboard' ethics.

These of course are more appropriate and convenient to pragmatic systems, (such as politics), where often they are inbuilt. True virtues, though often appropriated and portrayed in the political arena, are nonetheless in dire short supply. While many politicians would carry affectation of virtue, in open view they too frequently display manifest ignorance in this regard. While we may well expect to meet *ethical* politicians, the *virtuous* one borders on the extinct.

Generally, politics are exposed to this by their attraction to pragmatics. They chiefly contemplate only transient phases of life experience alone, (often devoid of true virtue). Too often are men subjected only to what ethics suggest, at best, given the power of those holding political leadership. Even in a spiritual desert this can at least carry the *appearance* of order. Politics are more speculative than inquisitorial. As Popper claims, the politician acts from 'a supposed knowledge of the future course of history', while there is no such knowledge. The same cannot be claimed of artists who were the driving force of mid twentieth century cultural rebellion in this nation, against a repressive society of different ilk, though armed with little more than an *intuitive feeling*, but a worthy and honest one at that.

Whatever inept law may issue from politics of fanciful idealism and confused thinking, man retains the potential to be resolved, at peace, and content with truths and a reality, far beyond the reach of *any* arrogant world leadership, or unjust law, derived of this. No more is this epitomised than in the words of Oscar Wilde, when he declares 'stone walls do not a prison make, nor iron bars a cage'. Our true solace lies with sufficient order of mind within, and not with some external mechanism that is without. All politics are mechanistic. It is by order of mind that we redeem ourselves, not by clutching some handbook of 'mechanics' of this ilk, and it is in the revelations of heroes in arts and sciences, tempered by wisdom, that this is most clearly apodeictic. We have no notion of past celebrities of their time in sport or mediocre entertainment, while much is recorded for posterity of artists, philosophers, and even generals.

Recognising where now we are is a necessary first step to reaching beyond it, as I hope now to show in the following chapter. Often are we all in the same pause of enigmatic wonder as Ophelia puts it so well; 'we know what we are, but know not what we may be', and I hope to offer a broad glimpse of this in what follows.

Forms and True Reality

Chapter 3 – Bodies and Shadows

The intelligibility principle and its implied eternal mind.
What we 'may be' must be inferred from what we 'are'.

Bertrand Russell rightly makes the remark that experience alone is insufficient to gathering whole knowledge; that because we cannot *see* the dark side of the moon, and we cannot have experience of it, nonetheless, this does not mean that it is not there. It follows, he rightly claims, that unless we make inference from, and often *beyond*, what we can experience, we can know very little apart from ourselves.

It is by the same token of obligatory inference, we are drawn to conclude that bodily satisfaction and what our *experience of life* presents to us, imminently, is insufficient to whole personhood; while it is true that what we are capable of *knowing about ourselves*, enriches us, at the same time what we experience gives opportunity to explore what is not 'us'. More than life experience is required to reach conviction that we amount to anything meaningful.

Often this arises by what appeals from *without*, (not necessarily something we can *see*), as much as it does by something we feel from *within*. At its broadest, we may describe this as a communion between some internal disembodied twin companion of our body, (our psyche is clearly *not* our body), and all of the true things beyond and outside it, which even reason tells us is, self-evidently, something greater than anything bodily we each *alone* signify.

In addition we are obliged to feel that this vastly greater thing than us somehow internally *requires* us, so that we are inclusive to it, and we loosely recognise this when we speak of 'nature' generally. From our experience then, we have little option but to infer that there is more to each of us than 'meets the eye', and that inference *from* what we experience is necessary. Further, it is entirely reasonable that we *make* such inference, even though clearly often it must lie *beyond* what we can experience.

Traditionally, this 'twin' is referred to as our spirit. Imaging of this concept is presented in the cover to this book. In my first work in this Philosophy of Feeling theme, I hope to have made a strong case for the integrity of such a 'spirit', but for the reader who may be unfamiliar with this, briefly I revisit that case here.

Though they cannot be seen, and must be *ascertained*, there are, self evidently, virtues, things which some object to as having no autonomy of their own. This is witnessed in the abandonment of the means of attaining them, by cherishing codes of morality. Instead of values derived of virtues, standards of correctness offered by the vagaries of 'ethics', or socially contrived mores of some sort are adopted. The true origin or incentive to values is put aside or 'bracketed'.

The obtaining in truth of the virtues is not in question here. The human individual has innate predilection for goodness as something cherished and loved for its own sake, even though some individuals on occasion fall short of achieving it, and castigate both their own shortcomings and those of others. This 'goodness' to which we are impelled, constitutes the virtues as generally subscribed to by world faiths, but there is as much argument for their being things of autonomous or intrinsic *a priori* knowledge, or merely that this is a condition of human being. Whatever their precise origin, virtues command and control our lives and will not be ignored; however they may be regarded as abstractions.

Hence the origin of law making, however diverted into ethic 'tributaries'. When troubled by our failures we refer to 'conscience', (and contemplate not public shame first, but *private guilt* first), aware of our better nature requiring goodness, as a distinctly *primary* thing to rightness. At root this is merely a *feeling* of which we are made aware, (by the feeling I describe above of our relation with something greater than us), and though intuitive, it can bring much discomfort from any conflict between our thoughts and our actions having contrary purpose. Similarly, clinging to virtues also, can bring bodily inconvenience and discomfort, and ultimately it is in the gravity of appeal, and the choices we make, whether we find ourselves with the *least* discomfort, or the most.

What we cannot deny, however, in this weighing of two contrary demands, directions offering choices of most appeal, the comfort and ease of the body, or an unfailing grasp of virtue informing the mind, (regardless of bodily inconvenience). This presents two distinct agendas, by two distinct commanders of action, and these are self-evident. The demands of both are true and real, and it is a condition of human experience that both must be recognised and then reconciled.

The companionship throughout life of spirit is not seriously challenged at all by Kant, as would be suggested, when in his Dreams of a Spirit Seer, he targets the more mystic work of Swedenborg, raising the question of how it can be possible for 'spirit' to be *at* an instant, *in* a place, and *during* a time. He did so anyway without the benefit of modern theoretical physics, and was pronouncing at a time of no 'Big Bang', no Singularity, no Black Holes, and space-time not itself reliably perceived as finite with a 'beginning'. There is no reliable support either in his time for the possibility of as many as ten dimensions of *being* in our living room, along with ourselves. Nor is he alone in creating doubt on the existence of things *unseen*.

Gilbert Ryle's input to philosophy has been said to have led to the remark that a thing is only real 'if you can hit it with a hammer', which I regard as not a remark to be taken too seriously. What may be conceived as some 'ghost within' is anathema to him. Neither can we be so outrageous as Zeno is said to have been, claiming that 'truth' is a 'solid'. It weighs nothing, has no odour, no shape, and is neither hot nor cold. Yet it *is* something, which clearly Zeno was wishing to emphasise. This concept of something 'real' though it cannot be perceived as something instanced in the sensory and physical world, is too frequently abused purely on the grounds that it is 'only a concept', and thereby uncertain. We cannot see feelings, but are obliged to accept their significance. Similarly, we may find ourselves obliged to embrace concepts, not as reflexive results of external stimuli, as Ryle would suggest, but as objects of very serious destination to very proactive acts of thought.

That also he raises the issue that if acts of will are voluntary, they are likely to be caused by previous acts of will, and so on, leading to regression, is untenable. It denies the unique character of private will and intentionality, any creative spiritual input of significance that fires it, along with any intuitive or predilective mindset. This is to underestimate the nature of the creative will, its independence and autonomy, and private interests that lend it force. Ryle's arguments have the affect of reducing human spirit to the level of mindless automation, and constitute a notion of despair inevitable as a consequence of uncritically embracing materialism.

Even the very title of Gilbert Ryle's major work presents *mind* as merely an academic bye product and *concept*, reducing it to the status of a collection point for neurological and material stimuli that in turn promotes mechanistic behavioural response. On the contrary, for Anaxagoras, over two millennia before him, *mind*, (deliberation), is the primary and eternal intelligible underpinning of all things, (motion, time, and change included). This is much more *a vital organ of dynamic responsibility* for all true being of anything, (the logos), including, (while explaining), human intelligence and self identity, (dismissed by Ryle as some ghost in a machine). This intelligibility runs throughout all things including man himself.

Combine with this Aristotle's description of an abstract entity of mind that bridges with understandings and abstractions, and the more recent comment of Bertrand Russell that it is responsible for 'our knowledge of all that is abstract and calculable', (a sort of magistrate of what is tenable), and we have the irony of the very thing Ryle intends to abuse when he speaks of a 'ghost in the machine' emerging with far greater likelihood of being a truth. I have by no means exhausted the intellective weight that so heavily strains the biological and psychological arguments of Ryle to breaking point. Epistemology, an avenue of philosophy concerning private thought and self resolution, is the parent of psychology, so that the fact that philosophic inquiry brings broader benefit than a derivative psychology, should not surprise.

The concept is not at times like this treated as anything objective or meaningful. It is claimed that a concept is the *possession* of a private mental 'object' which, I am persuaded, is 'going before one's horse to market'. A concept is never possessed, for, as we see, there is nothing in the mind but an 'act of thinking' as Russell declares. It is directed *at* an object *beyond* the mind. A concept is not therefore primarily a *possession*, but an *object accessed* by the act of thought.

The underlying truth that Zeno does emphasise, is that to reveal, realize, or conceive, of 'things' of truth and reality, which may have no physical *existence* in the sensory world, is neither erroneous, nor fictional, for they have undeniable metaphysical *being* and presence. The notion of 'reification', making abstract things *seem* concrete, has no place here in the face of what actually pertains. Unseen entities, such as truth and beauty are just as necessary as any material 'objects of furniture' in the world, if ever sensibly and intelligently it is disclosed to us and we are to apprehend it. Zeno was indeed right to those who *know* him to be for he speaks within the remit of the principle of intelligibility.

This is a good introduction to distinguishing that there are two kinds of 'things' in the world; those that *are* solid, like a tree or a boulder, and those that are not, like truth or beauty. While a tree may be *seen*, and we may physically engage with a boulder, if we are to encounter, (instead of an object of thing, like a boulder), an object of truth, we must reason, so to *ascertain* it, or it must, in some way, be revealed to us.

All men may distinguish truth, so that its *being* is never in question, in spite of never *experiencing* it as a sensation of sight, touch, or smell. It is ubiquitous however invisible. Some say they have it though they cannot be believed, while others believe they have it when they do not, and still others, knowing they do or do not have it, hide this privately or publicly, where it brings them some advantage. This creates much confusion in its wake. Clearly we *ascertain* many true, though unseen, things, as *real*, though there may *exist in life*, nothing physically present in time and space by which they are manifested. No triangles are found in flower gardens. By this fact, the materialist or the empiricist is enabled to choose the unchallenging path of selectively dismissing truths not to his liking, those he cannot see or touch, as mere meaningless abstractions unworthy of serious consideration.

In any serious attempt, however, to establish this scenario of a *Two Worlds Theory*, the World of Sensibility, and that of Intelligibility, it is important to avoid distinguishing them as *entirely* apart and unrelated to each other as we shall later see. The world of experience repeatedly refers, or leads to, the other.

In the field of experience, or living, the two have a synchronicity, such that human individuals may have a 'foot in each camp' so to speak, by means of the duality of human identity. There is the camp of physical *existence*, and that of spiritual *being*; the first engaging with phenomena in time and space, and with *life* and *existence*, the second with spiritual and contemplative objectives, of private interest. The work of sculptors exemplifies this; physical form identifying spiritual 'substance' or significance.

In truth, we are condemned to a schizophrenic outlook on this account, for we are each leading two forms of vitalism, though many of us ignore it. Objectives of our *being* are unchained to any particular place at any given time, and are with the unchanging and rigid *constant* of *truth and being*, much as presented by Gabriel Marcel in his work *Etre et Avoir,* and as outlined in my first book in the Philosophy of Feeling series.

Intelligible objects to our thought, and which we contemplate, whether or not there is *instance* of them in the physical world, often present as qualified 'truths', though we are at liberty to ignore them when we choose. Nevertheless, we must *encounter* them, for they are clear objects to which thought is directed, and *are* something, however non-material they may be. Encountering them is a required facet of our *being,* and that, in turn, is also a requirement, though fragmentary, of the wholeness and unity of all that is greater and beyond us, because, as we have seen, we are inclusive to it.

It is *at* a place and *in* a time that we experience sensible 'objects', boulders, trees, or our fellows, but, as objects of intelligibility, at *any* place and at *any* time, (which *includes* particular places and instants), they are intelligible objects of *contemplation.* We are empowered *always* to engage with, or to *ascertain* them. All we have to distinguish is the difference of *presence* this poses between the *seen* and the *ascertained,* (or even the revealed).

Clearly it must be born in mind that while *presence* of an object of *intelligibility,* the *ascertained,* may remain undiscovered for any indefinite period, the same cannot be said of the 'face to face' encounter with the *presence* of an object of *sensibility, or* the *seen,* and, having immediacy, cannot be avoided. It follows that any sensible object carries with it as a matter of course, (like a shadow), its relation, its intelligible object, and always this remains accessible to thought and contemplation. We can think again of the small boulder over which we tripped. Where true and real it must conform to the intelligible principle. We may just as easily *contemplate* our father as we may *encounter* him. His physical presence in the world is simply not required for the former.

Presence, as a sensible object, solid and material, and within boundaries of time, space, and general physics, may, as truth and reality, be open to question, and for two important reasons. It may be counterfeit by way of illusion, or perceptually deceiving. Secondly, however *physically* substantive a sense object, chained within the boundaries referred to above, (and therefore following the dynamic 'arrow of time' towards entropy), reliably, and predictably, it must end. It cannot *endure* as a sense object, by physics, sufficiently to qualify, (by the durability expected of truth and reality), *always* to pertain. It can indeed, by these means, certainly and must cease to exist. Its counterpart, however, as intelligible *object of contemplation*, has extension, as we shall see. It is not its physics that authenticate it as anything true and real.

Presence as intelligible object occurs as an obligatory counterpart to a sensible object, (object of conceiving as against object of perceiving). Even any object of which there is *no* sensible counterpart instanced in the world, and contemplated *only* by act of thought, or by some procedure of reasoning, *is always,* regardless and independently of physics, time and space. It must endure, and *never* ends, however we may, or may not, *perceive* any sensible counterpart to which it is allied. Not contained by a mind, but outside it, it does not end. Unlike the sensible object, the intelligible object, independently and self evidently, qualifies as a fixed, rigid, and unchangeable truth and reality. This of course cannot apply to the *deliberately fictional object* that is untrue and *known* to be so in advance. Creative writing manipulates this fact.

The live Napoleon is both sensible *and* intelligible, while at the same time things of the sensible world are intelligible *to* him. The dead one *remains* always intelligible, as a human individual, *to* the sensible world, but has no longer any *internal relation* to sensible things, or the present moment in time, and there can be no physical sign that things are continuing to be intelligible to *him.*

Things of the sensory physical world are no less intelligible, true, and real, than are 'things' of intelligibility which are not material, such as beauty or goodness. What they share is truth and reality. This sharing of all-inclusive truth and reality firmly underpins a relation between what is physical and what is not. This is how we show that there is indeed a relation between a human individual, (whether he is living or not), any apple past or present, the Battle of Trafalgar, and whiteness. All share the relation to truth and reality. But this can only be an *external* relation where each does not require the other to be exactly what it is. We see from this that while the dead Napoleon is denied any internal relation to sensible things, (the physical presence of each *required* by the other), he always *must* have an external one to them.

This further clarifies why physical encounter with 'things' is simply not necessary for us to know them to be true and real, provided they are of singular and intelligible identity. Any particular object in the world, such as a boulder, must be, as a sensible object, intelligible to the mind of an observer. It is not however intelligible to itself. But for the observer, as an intelligible object, it can be contemplated *any* time, whether or not it is actually present as a sensible object.

Napoleon can contemplate the boulder because it *is* an intelligible *as well as* a physical thing, *and*, because it is intelligible *to him*. This is an *internal relation* with the sensible world. When dead, however, he continues to have *external* relation with *all* true things, whether or not he knows of them in his *living and existing* time. Essentially this is because his personhood is inclusive to the sum of all truth.

It is quite a different case for the boulder however, for having no 'mind', it is never intelligible to *itself* any more than are other 'things', including Napoleon. This we may call a *simple relation* of intelligibility, (as it applies to a boulder), for it can only present as an intelligible object *to* an observer or contemplator, having no awareness of itself or anything else. In the direction of any observer 'mind' however, it is intelligible, *physical or not*. Though it is *required* that it is intelligible as a 'boulder' so to *exist*, as a sense object, *or* as one that is contemplated, (as an *intelligible* object), the mind of the observer, as with Napoleon, is *required* for this, if it is to be realised.

Not only can Napoleon *observe* the boulder, he can also *contemplate* it, which renders him double purchase on the *one* intelligible object. This is a *complex* relation with the intelligibility principle. While the boulder simply *is* intelligible, he can *see it or think* it, intelligibly. This is what distinguishes the animate from the inanimate, and the active or passive function of the intelligibility principle.

What qualifies both Napoleon *and* the boulder, as true and real, is their relation, simple or complex, with intelligibility *at all*. By way of contrast with the *personhood* of Napoleon, a boulder that he may have stepped over has no complex relation of intelligibility, is entirely passive, and is intelligible only in simple dimension, namely for any observer, or anyone who contemplates it by an act of thought in his mind (and whether the boulder is actually present or not). The boulder *cannot* contemplate Napoleon, in spite of, itself, being an intelligible and sensible object. It is 'mindless'. Therefore it has no *mental life*.

What distinguishes Napoleon's and the boulder's obliged relation to the principle of intelligibility, underwriting the truth and reality relation of both, is that in Napoleon's case it is active and animated, and therefore complex, while for the boulder, it is passive and inanimate, and therefore simple. All else, (things 'other', or alterity), is intelligible *to* Napoleon. By way of contrast, the boulder is intelligible to all else, while *nothing* is intelligible to the boulder. This is a *simple* relation with intelligibility.

The avenue of access to which I refer above for Napoleon, (if we speculate he should *have* such private interests in sensible 'things' *after* his existence as he had *during* it), still to enjoy military expeditions *after* his lifetime, it is by his relation of external variety with truth and reality. This is an entirely plausible bridging of separated things being bound together by a unifying principle. Both are informed of, or infused by, the intelligibility principle. This is something quite distinct from experiences of living and existing bereft of mental life. Objectives of mental life mediate with the realm of *being* (true and real). Awareness of the unseen is commonplace to it.

As an interesting 'aside', it is reasonable to infer from this that Napoleon's dreams, (encounters distinguishable from physical life experience), and which no boulder can have, are likely to be some significant bridging between the *perceivable*, and the *conceivable*. It is a sort of dialogue between our consciousness and our unconscious. To whatever degree dreams can be significant however can only be effective in proportion to what the will allows, as they engage with a sense of experiences often far removed from the pragmatics of physical life experience. At the same time, the fact that they can prove ultimately to be *predictive* of events, which later occur, merely reinforces the notion that what *is* bridged are very true and real zones bridging sensory *life experience*, and nonsensory *intelligible being*.

So is it that we are enabled to distinguish two categories of objects; those *seen* and those *ascertained*. Both have an equivalence of claim on truth and reality. Plato concludes from this basis that there are the two very separated worlds, one of *appearance*, and one of *reality*, but goes further by attributing provenance, credentials and authenticity for objects that are sensible, (and by such means as *universals*), to their *derivation* from the intelligible world, highlighting that sensible objects are no more than representations of something truly 'other', when it comes to truth and reality.

This emphasis implies that sense objects, *representations*, only qualifying as authentic from the intelligible world, are therefore somewhat dismissive and inconsequential. They are no more than imagery. It is not the boulder, for example, which is truly *real*, but the 'boulderness' universal, (class of like things), from which it is derived. This intensely spiritual or mystic view excludes altogether the possibility of anything of the sensible world being inclusive to any total of *all true things*, although it must be so. The boulder above that Napoleon steps over, although it cannot be an active intelligible object, is certainly a passive one, and constituent to any reality as a whole. It is not required to have mental life. I am persuaded Plato's mystic emphasis is only supportable in a scenario where 'duality' of body and spirit disregards the body *altogether*, in favour of the 'truth' of the spirit. The body in this context is *nothing at all*. I am persuaded this is untenable.

In theological terms this is often misconstrued as authorised by Christian scripture, when in fact it is not. When Jesus says, for example, 'the spirit is life, the flesh is nothing', clearly by 'flesh' He refers to the human body which without it's spirit can have no personhood, no real identity, and would be unintelligible as anything meaningful, and the 'duality', or 'two in one', to which in other contexts Jesus refers, is emphasised. Theologians have so often trumpeted this misunderstanding over the centuries that they create more confusion by what it implies. Jesus did not say 'physical things are nothing', and it takes little scrutiny to see how wrong they are. If physical things, (including individual human presence in the physical form of a body), are indeed nothing, and if it is given God created *all* things, God has *also* created *nothing*, which is quite absurd.

That the body of a human individual should be considered nothing, is, however, a grim, fatalistic, and determinist scenario as any sort of model. Neither is it compatible with 'duality' of body and spirit, where body and spirit may become the 'two in one' of which Jesus speaks, and it makes little sense. The complex entity is necessarily composed of two otherwise differing ones.

If the body, (or a boulder also), is a mere 'appearance' or representation of something *elsewhere*, (as Plato would have it), then it, and anything it implements, is wholly meaningless, for it's meaning rests with something else elsewhere, rendering it in truth not an entity at all, but a relation. It has no significance itself, and no true consequence issues from it, and something other bears responsibility for it. Even to the practicing Christian, whose resultant '*eternal life*' is consequent to how the body has been directed, or conducted itself, must find such an understanding wholly absurd. All consequence of the life experience of human individuals in this scenario, whether saint or sinner, is nothing then, (life experience having no significance of its own). There is no purpose to it, and it is an absurdity.

After all, and as Russell suggests, even an *appearance* must be *of* something, and, if not illusory, this is something inclusive to truth and reality. A body may be an object as a phenomenon, *or* as a noumenon. This is so *by* its *intelligibility* as an object of either kind. With the passing away or degeneration of a phenomenal 'thing', the fact that it has extension of any sort by way of the noumena to which it is 'wed', does not, in my view, require a literal 'place', intelligible world-warehouse, where 'prototype' noumena stand in waiting on shelves.

Speaking precisely of 'two worlds', we do not have to think of two worlds that share *nothing*, or are wholly 'divorced' from each other, (they share truth and reality), but two zones of distinctive properties, one sensory and the other supersensory. All that is required of the physical object to have extension as object to thought, (even the spirit or soul of a human individual), is that it shares the *property* of intelligibility. This constitutes a coherent identity, which can *transcend* as 'object to thought' at any time, and where *always* it is then accessible. What is intelligible is worthy of belief.

The alternative scenario of two worlds, enabling 'duality' to which I subscribe, is that of a human individual *living* an experiential life, *while being* simultaneously spiritually vital and aware. The one is subject to entropy and degenerates, while the other has no physics and cannot. This does not mean the *living* human individual is unreal, or untrue, but, on the contrary, because he *is* real and true, (intelligible), his 'living' can only be an *incomplete explanation* of him.

That living *is* an incomplete explanation of a human individual is not some notion grasped out of thin air. Neither is it based upon a blind faith that we each have some ethereal 'spirit'. The truth of the case I make rests upon the wholly reasonable argument that if a thing is a truth it cannot become *not* a truth, is unchangeable, (and therefore beyond space and time), and is obliged *always* to obtain without interference, or any sort of influence *by* these dimensions. It is a stasis of durability entirely beyond the control of physics, (which of course *requires* the metaphysic, or 'beyond physics', principle). There can be no *life* within the principle, but there is *being*, (of which Gabriel speaks in 1935), and, furthermore, it is clear that it is *intelligible to us* in spite of its distanced, though *required* relation, to practical living.

What, for example, Christian philosophy underwrites, is the foolishness of ignoring *duality*, and focusing entirely on the senses receptive to physical life, while ignoring spiritual need, or living 'like a brick'. On any day of our life experience, however we spend it, we enrich it or impoverish it by our attention or otherwise to our being 'two in one', and inhabiting the 'two worlds' of which I speak.

The equivalence of claim for physical and spiritual presence, the perceived or the conceived, the seen or the ascertained, is sustained by a common intelligibility. Rather than choosing to adopt the model of some *place* beyond physics, an intelligible 'world', this is greater recognition of the *principle* of intelligibility. It is by intelligibility that *all* things have credentials, and by this common property they can be considered true and real.

Even our boulder cannot be denied inclusion, even if only on the basis of its passive existence to the senses, (and lacking the duality which spirituality confers), for it is its intelligibility raises it to the noumenal plane, as object to thought, not any active 'self' which is not in its gift. There can be no love-founded Paradise for it to reach, for it has no love, and no will to action. While it is a *passive* intelligible *thing*, it has no *active* vital spirit or will.

All 'things', whether physical and therefore phenomena, or immaterial, as objects only to thought, and noumena, compose the Sigma, as I refer to it in the first book of this series, or the sum total of all that can ever be true and real. The *Absolute idea* as Hegel puts it. Bluebells, boulders, or bodies, are intelligible objects of physics in the sensory world open to acts of perception, just as much as they are to acts of conception. By the property of intelligibility they have passive extension, but as material 'things', bluebells and boulders, unlike human individual bodies, have no capacity for duality, or active autonomous and independent *being* or spirit.

They have no ultimate resolution and rest *except* as passive commodities or inanimate 'things' feeling nothing about anything. Without spirit, they cannot revise or review themselves, or contemplate what is about them. Nonetheless, as intelligible objects, they are true and real and inclusive to Hegel's absolute idea, or the sum total of all truths.

This gift of *spirit* in the active human individual, (missing in the case of material things without self-awareness), further supports the comforting notion that the appearance of our fathers in the world, if they are at all true and real, and, incidentally, their departure from it, leaves their true *being*, (spirit or personhood), *required independently* of physical things which once their bodies displayed. But our fathers are *active* things, wholly true and real, while boulders are *inactive* 'things' having only intelligible and dependent extension by their truth and reality of *physical* variety. This self-defines *them*, in contrast to fathers, as passive 'commodities'. Both our fathers *and* boulders, however distinct, are, nonetheless, extensive by their required core of intelligibility authenticating them.

The principle of intelligibility is the interrelation between *all* 'things', as we may observe the knots tied in a continuous cord, which is another way of speaking of the logos, or the sigma. Without the integrity of this principle bestowed upon *all* entities, there is no meaning or sense, for it is this that provides authenticity and credentials to all meaningful things. No individual knot gives us an accurate explanation of the whole cord with all its knots.

Aristotle touches on one of the benefits we inherit from this, in that what we feel, our emotions, are guided by the same intelligibility that informs us of ourselves and all that surrounds us. It is an underpinning order to everything, and not confined to physics. The Stoics wholly embraced this notion. Philo, a contemporary of Jesus, defines the logos as the '*divine articulation in all nature and human intelligence*'. While time enables us while *living and experiencing*, to perceive things in a place or at a distance, it does not in any way affect their, (or our), *being*. That is an alternative class of true and intelligible things, submissive to the web of interrelation, between *all* things; the one principle of intelligibility. We ourselves, whether as *living things* or *beings*, are fragments to the same principle informing *all* things.

Charles Pierce contributes greatly to the same notion in highlighting how all things present to us in a state of 'firstness', as a thing, but 'secondness' coming into it when we are aware of its relations, to many *other* things, and, further, that the mediator in this procedure is a 'thirdness', or the *meaning and intelligibility* that permeates all three. A 'logos' again emerges.

In the Zeno sense of exaggerated 'solidity' then, any 'thing', phenomenal *or* noumenal, that is 'full bodied' and *inherent to the core of intelligibility*, (demonstrated by a knotted rope), has integrity of meaning whether abstract or tactile, and is true, real, and perpetual. Change, (or time), is in this context, meaningless.

Our scrutiny of the boulder and Napoleon, their passive simple, and, active complex, dependent relation on intelligibility, respectively, has implications of its own of course. Even in the case of our 'mindless' and inanimate boulder, we discern a *true* anchor of reliable integrity, under the principle of intelligibility. It is both sensible and intelligible, as distinct *forms* of *one* thing, (deprived of the intelligible one it could neither *exist* nor *be*). This is *more* suggestive of *deliberate intent* and a commanding will than it is of any random or coincidental system, where the foundational cord implies mental life of some dimension by the intrinsic skill of its order. A solution to this question may well evolve as we proceed.

For now we may simply note that the time lapse that astronomers use to see the birth and death of stars is carried by light over immense distances measuring light years. What happened, 250 million years ago, we know nothing of until its consequence; light taking time to traverse a distance of space revealing a truth to us. It is the consequence of the light emitted by the event that makes the event itself intelligible to us, though we have no hope ever of observing *at* the measurable moment of time of its inception.

The material things measurable by time, space and its boundaries of physics, preclude the experience. But to be intelligible at all *to us* it is required that it is itself intelligible to begin with, so that, though at some length, we can apprehend it. It is the intelligibility principle informs both it, and our apprehension of it. It is the principle that authenticates the true being of anything.

The light, time and space involved, are not the event, but consequent of it. It is from the true being of the event that all consequence follows. Both the truth of the event, and the truth of its consequences, are distinguishable and separate things, though they share common authenticity grounded in intelligible truth, and are associated with a particular thing of identity. It is intelligibility that is the mediator between any intelligible thing and its intelligent observer. Each seems to require the other. In any matter of truth, even without any tactile phenomenon, as in the case of an idea, this is commonplace. The human body is consequent of an individual's true being, a consequence of truth being that *is* observable.

Time, space, and light, are attributes and properties related to the being of true substance and actuality that is the event or happening, and even the human individual. The physics bespeak of something that is of true being. The truth of the intelligible event, and its intelligible consequences, has intellective binding by relation to the authenticity of their origination in truth. Origination, (what some may call creation), constitutes the thread of the intelligibility principle informing all actuality, reality, or the sum of all true things. It cannot, perversely, be *unintelligible* in nature.

It is an entirely reasonable inference to make from here that the origin of an intelligible event, (whether we speak of the reader or the universe), if it is to exist in any sense at all, and because of all its complex and necessary integral requirements to pertain, cannot be other than intellective in nature. All things require intelligible subframe or grounding typifying intellective life of some variety. What 'typifies' unending truths this way are such things as deliberation, intentionality, and will. No finite mental life, as we readily recognise, is sufficient in its truth being, (changeless and unending), either to support an intellective creator, or any real thing created by it as 'being' of unending truth. Only infinite mental life is sufficient to such higher echelons of intellective mediation.

Quite apart from inception, everything, even chemical interaction, requires a mediating energiser or *agency* for activation, or there can be nothing. Self-vitalising, and self-energising random event is proscribed by its very deficiency. Without devising and intention it cannot be. There is an *intellective knowing of all that can be*, (somewhere), if what we observe *is* intelligible. As Parmenides reminds us, there is no 'knowing' of 'what is not'.

To apprehend this, we have the support of two things for our reasoning so to be justified. There is the 'superimposition of states' as refered to by Schrodinger's Cat, where more than one state of a thing is the norm in quantum mechanics, whereas to observation always there is only one state, though which state it can be *when* observed cannot be predicted. The thought experiment concerns the 'cat in a box' with a phial of gas that will break, if and only if, the decay of a radium atom is registered by it. Between the cat and the devise there is a 'superposition of states', and if the phial is broken the cat will be dead. The superimposition of states establishes the cat is either live or dead. This pertains only until there is an observer of whether the cat is alive or dead when one state or the other will be determined. Without the observer, the life or death of the cat remains indeterminate.

The multi-stated thing, (a thing of truth), though observed only in one state, is intelligible within quantum, *in whichever state*, and even the condition of being multi-stated is intelligible to us, though it seems to suggest a paradox. In accord with my overall theme, and though not a precise analogy, we may feel similarly on encountering a corpse, that we are confronted by a 'superposition of states', only one of which can be observed. All that is observed is a body, (due to the observer's natural boundaries of physics to which any spirit identifiable with that body is unobservable). Yet we may readily subscribe to such a spirit as plausible if our philosophic attitude allows.

It is no more possible to observe any mediating agency 'pulling the strings of the states', in the case of our corpse, any more than it is in the case of Schrodinger's Cat, though in either case we are dealing with opposing outcomes, both of which are intelligible. This implies responsibility of authorship, of what is both observable and what is not, and that requires intelligence. The event is required to be intelligible, while simultaneously intelligible to us. Some sort of extraneous mediating agency of 'thirdness', of intellective power, with independent input in either case, is implied by the whole scenario; a force we are veiled from grasping.

What reinforces this is the Argument of Sufficient Reason of Leibniz. Whatever state something is in, live cat or dead cat, father or corpse, there must be sufficient reason, for the states themselves, for though intelligible, they are an incomplete and insufficient explanation of what is observed, for we cannot apprehend the missing 'superimposition' stage of states. The 'thirdness' required *is* the veiled sufficient reason and missing completeness.

What is clearly suggested is intellective mediation and agency, beyond our grasp as may be. Omniscient force or control of some hierarchal intellective order would seem to be necessary, all of which is persuasively convergent with the myriad compossibility that is so commonplace, and all of which is intelligible. There is a sort of superimposed web of cogent outcomes. This obligates us only prudently to adopt what is reasonably inferred, a hierarchical 'high command' of some sort that is intellective. What is intellective demands abstraction and thought. A further bonus to recognition of this is the universal *intellective knowing*, to which I refer above, in that it requires no further explanation as a matter of course.

In the chapters to follow in this book, an attempt is made to assemble a comprehensive expectation that while the *Two Worlds Theory* of the sensible *and* the intelligible object is justified for the purpose of distinguishing sensory presence from supersensory significance, on reasoned grounds, so also is the Hegelian notion convergent, in that all constituent elements of both must necessarily be inclusive to the *Absolute Idea*.

Chapter 4 – Neither here nor there, but both

Distinguishing the created from the inferred; the discerned and the knowable.
Creativity and the resource of superimposition.

Our viewpoint requires that when we speak of 'two worlds' we are observer of one from another, and while living and experiencing this reduces to viewing the metaphysical from the physical. It is solely then by inference that we are enabled to distinguish the *physical and passing,* from *lasting,* things of truth.

The one from which we observe passes, and appeals to us as very much 'here', and *very* 'real', while the other must present as something removed and 'there'. This stems from the immediacy of the world of sense, with its abundance and variety of what is concrete and tactile all about us. Whatever presents to us as non-material, abstract, and only accessible with the labour of some reasoning, or act of thinking, *intelligible,* though somewhere else, is *without* the tactile properties familiar to us. Naturally in these circumstances, it presents as *at a distance* and difficult to engage with in the usual way that we can experience things.

This distinction of *separation* however, is, in any meaningful way, artificial, and does not encourage us to see the undeniable synchronicity between the two. What is bound by the principle of intelligibility binds *all* things, empowering all of them to be true and real. In life and existence, what is living and existing, if true and real, is primarily intelligible. If it is that, it is *bound with* intelligible things of inference, that do *not* live or exist, but *have being* as truth, however abstracted from sensible things.

Though some may be unaware of it, and others exclude it as a possibility from the outset, and Bertrand Russell admits of it, both worlds, of sense objects and of intelligible objects, (the *seen,* and the *ascertained*), 'are real, and have the *same* claim on our impartial attention'. We are obliged to conduct even our conscious and very physical lives *here* in relation to *both.*

It follows that we are obliged to conduct our lives by engagement both with acts of perceiving *and* acts of conceiving, (or as suggested earlier, *accessing*), in order that the relation between what is sensible and what is intelligible makes a consistent weave of our 'lifescape'. Two Worlds, as posited by Plato, as the one of appearance and the one of reality, and by Aristotle, as more the one of physics and that of metaphysics, in addition to those purported by Christianity, that of the mortal and that of the immortal offer varying scope. However differing these notions may be thought to be, nonetheless, the *two* worlds of the *seen* and the *ascertained* are rightly perennial and received as given.

To some extent this balance is distorted in some world faiths when it comes to a matter of theology. By undue emphasis on 'the world to come', to near dismissal of the sensory world as nothing much more than a 'veil of tears', (though as earlier suggested we lead both spiritual *and* physical dimensions simultaneously while living), some are discouraged. They prefer, as they say, more to dwell with the business of 'this world' that is *known* to them, than to hope for some future world which is *not*, and which they are expected intellectively to intuit, or feel things about. Generally they feel they can *know* little *here* of some such remote place.

Theology carries more constructive a route where it declares that adherents should conduct themselves in a manner such that they are fully aware of their duality; that they are obliged to engage with both what is sensible *and* what is intelligible, and *now*. This induces a relation of synchronicity between the *here* and the *there*. A human individual does not have merely to *endure* life here, with some vague spirit life far ahead at some appointed future place somewhere, when already he engages with both *now*. This apperception leads to that balance of emotion and intellect so recommended by Thomas More, promoting equanimity and well being, with a view to what is perceived as a *daily* awareness ideally running parallel to a spiritually informed and ordered life.

The view of *two* worlds we have while in the one that we describe as *here*, and about us, given the circumstances of our sensory surrounds, is most readily characterised in the way I suggest, as that which is *seen*, rather than that which is *ascertained*. Our knowledge of the physical world in time and space is largely the result, though not wholly, of our direct acquaintance with it, requiring mostly simply the gathering of 'sense data'. As Russell puts it, 'we speak of things *existing* when they are in time, that is to say, we can point to some time *at* which they *'exist'*. If we have no knowledge by acquaintance, we may know of them when we are informed by a reliable source.

This is not the same way, however, that we may know of things which are *not* here in the world of space and time, but *there*, removed from physics, space and time; that *other* world for which we have so many names dependent on our private interests, and about which we must form a judgement. We may refer to a supersensory world, the intelligible world, the spirit world, and so on. It is in that world *there* wherein things have *being* always, (and not *here* in the physical world), and again as Russell says, 'where *being* is opposed to *existence,* and is *timeless'*.

This intelligible world of *being* he says, 'is unchangeable, rigid, exact, delightful to the mathematician, the logician, the builder of metaphysical systems, etc., and a world we know is *there* somewhere, by reasoning, a wholly different way of discovery to that of *here,* in the sensible or sensory world.' Both are real Russell reiterates.

There are numerous ways of demonstrating how all of this is exactly so. There is no such thing, for example, as a definitive straight line in this world here, from which we speak, yet, by the approximation of three such lines, we may construct a 'non-existent' triangle, for it does not *exist* here, and by such means we can achieve many things *here* in this world, which, otherwise, would be impossible. The same may be said of the use of truth, or the pursuit of beauty. We may well ask how much we relied on 'non-existent' triangles to reach the moon. We can contemplate an idea, as object to our act of thought, (and a *concept*), independently of our place *here,* where it does not exist, from the point where we are sure of its *being* there, in spite of not *existing* here.

In the same way, in Russell's example, when we speak of Edinburgh being 'north of London', we apprehend a fact which was there already before we know it, and, 'where Edinburgh stands would be north of where London stands, even if there were no human being to know of north and south'. North, then, has no dependence on thought, and this truth or fact requires no human mental activity, but belongs to the *intelligible world* which 'thought and the mind apprehends, but does not create'. 'North of', he says, does not exist here, in the way that London most certainly does, and is different to things in 'space and time; neither *material nor mental'*, nevertheless, it is certainly an actuality *there.* This is a paradigm object of a concept not *possessed* by minds, though it may be *accessed.*

In another case Russell poses, he reminds us *universals* are things, which apply to collections. 'What many different thoughts of whiteness have in common is their *object,* and each man's object of thought will differ. Thus, universals are not thoughts', but are 'objects of thought'. Universals are not contained in minds, and at the same time, are 'not evident' here in the sensory world. Yet they are *something,* and are *somewhere,* though they do not *exist* here. They have *being,* which is *there.*

For those whose private interests contemplate a Creator, or God, again as object of thought, neither contained in minds, (not possessed privately in mind), nor evident here in time and space, similar approach of reasoning is necessary. We can grasp something that, though we intuit or feel it to have being there, has no *existence* here in the world of time and space. The idea is nonetheless obliged to *be* something, as Kant or Descartes may assert, and as universal object of thought to reasoning, intuited, reckoned, or simply 'felt', and however not existing here. It can only then be *there* that it may be placed, beyond the time and space of the sensible world *here.* It is precisely on the grounds that only what is *here* can be verified by physical means that the objection of the materialist stands, and yet, it cannot be within the 'brief' of physics to verify something which *has no physics,* though we know it *is* something.

Although it is with great eloquence, and much illumination, that Russell deals with 'problems of philosophy' in general, he imposes an inappropriate limit on knowledge in the case of 'acts of thought' and reasoning. He thinks we 'leap' too readily to sublime resolution in matters of metaphysics. He considers that before we may accept that in line with Hegel's thinking, a man's *nature* may be a part of, or inclusive, to the 'whole of all that can be', or the *Absolute Idea,* his *nature,* or all that makes him what he is, must first be comprehensively 'known'.

The received view of any man's nature is generally regarded as that which his personality and temperament, along with his private interests, compose. Therefore, it must also be received as something that is identifiable. It does not, however, require being identifiable in order to be that something that it is. It is something anyway, identified or not. It is therefore inclusive to the whole of everything. Russell's skewed reliance on predetermined and excessive knowledge of a man's *nature,* (a knowledge which Russell's own pre-existent 'relation' in Edinburgh being north of London, does *not* require), is simply not necessary for a man to be inclusive to the *Absolute Idea.*

A man, and his 'nature', is obliged to be parts to the whole of everything, regardless of what may become *known* of his nature. I hope to rely on this when I deal with what I refer to as a 'celestial beach'.

In the case of our beach then, itself infinite, there are infinite grains of sand, and while it is possible always to study, count, and inspect individual grains, and even heaps of them, always there are more, with which we can do nothing of the sort, and with which we can have no such familiarity. What we can know of the sand, as a whole, is obliged always to be incomplete, as is our knowledge of each grain.

We have to admit, of course, that this beach is a construct that is entirely notional, but even were we to consider a material beach instead, in the physical and sensory world, and on the west coast of Ireland for example, in practice, we are likely very much to confront the same difficulty, so that we cannot know every grain. Although the grains of sand are now finite, they are so vast in number that they may as well be infinite. In such circumstances, is it probable that ever we can expect to have intimate knowledge of all grains of sand? We share the same limitations that afflicted Archimedes when in an attempt to calculate all the grains of sand in the universe, not being acquainted with any boundaries, the best he could do was to provide a hypothesis based on a speculative universe.

Creatively, we have explored the possibility, pushing it to probability, that at least theoretically, there could be many things we cannot intimately know, and we can reliably expect that in practice, on our Irish beach, the same is the case. Whether what we contemplate is finite or infinite, we cannot know everything. We have found an object of thought, our notional beach, to suggest the same probable outcome by reasoning that is likely from any experiential encounter with an object of thing, or our Irish one.

The human condition allows of a propensity to ascertain what is convincingly likely to be a truth by thought alone, which in our case here, does not require that we stand on an Irish beach. It is sufficient to ascertain a probable truth without the necessity to see or *experience* it in a physically intimate way. Neither can we hope to see or ascertain the whole of all that can be, though intuitively, perhaps in an *a priori* way, we are empowered generally to anticipate there being such a 'whole', a Sigma, a sum total of all that *can* ever be. With such a notion we are exercising our propensity to ascertain a distinct probability. Although this, (the fact that there may *be* any sum total of all things), may at first seem little advance on the hypothesis of Archimedes above, it is in my own view extremely probable that it is the best solution we can reach.

It is clear that we are condemned to advancing with both the advantages and disadvantages of occupying two driving seats at once, which we do, preferably, while following a single direction. We must bring together what can be seen, with what can be ascertained, what can be thought, with what can be done, what is theoretical with what is practical, in some coherent way.

To lead meaningful lives we must draw together theory and practice into some self-consistent unity that has synchronicity. I am persuaded that the direction of greatest appeal for us all is that which ultimately unveils that unchangeable state of being, greater than life itself, to which the 'chain of being' of Plotinus, or the principle of intelligibility we have outlined, insistently leads. Leading meaningful lives is a position of rest and composure, brought about by the unity and self consistency of what we think and feel coming together, in the singularity of who and what we are. This may be achieved *while* living and experiencing.

We have as human individuals a capacity to *will* something, *in order* to contemplate it, as an object to our act of thinking. This is the power of creativity and imagination endowing things with a potential, plausibility, for wilful belief. As Shakespeare suggests, we must suspend our disbelief when imagination is employed. Unlike objects of thought arrived at by some revelatory procedure of meditation, or as the result of laboured reasoning, that reveal or uncover *truths*, of which we have little doubt, such objects of contemplation, as those willed, are contrived, without anything in support to suggest they are anything but fictional and untrue. They are wilful and imaginative counterfeits of truth. They are *preknown* to have no clear basis of truth like that of either reasoning or revelation, yet we *confer* a substitute truth upon them.

As it is only with groundless and empty beliefs is it usual that truth is conferred in such a way, (and as no truth may be contrived of falsehood), we are right to ask how, without any potential for true being, are we able at all *truly* to contemplate them, as authentic objects to acts of thought. It is clear that we fabricate by will *some* artificial sense of *being* for them in order for them authentically to be contemplated or acted upon. This raises a serious enquiry with regard to the Arts and the nature of creativity. Do we create what are potential things, (are they pre-existent to our creating them, and actual possibilities already), so that we are merely discovering their *true* being, as it were, or, are we, like God is thought to be, creating out of nothing?

An artist or composer is likely to argue that to define his life's work as falsehood and deceit, or something contrived and untrue, is something to be rejected. As in the case of reasoning or revelation, he must claim, any object he contemplates in his genre of work must have some form of *being*, (be intelligible and true), for him to contemplate it sufficiently and give it form. Likewise, the novelist will argue that he must be empowered to contemplate the object of his chief character, and that it has some sense of being and metaphysical truth, so that he can give *that* form also. Though it seems certainly the case that the artist, composer, and novelist, have 'imaginatively contrived' the objects of their work, and that it therefore can have no basis in factual or propositional claims of truth, there is good reason why this may *not* always be so. That reason rests with our underestimate of the creative will.

Things contemplated must have some sense of being to *be* contemplated, by thought, though they need not live or exist. It is true that works of art, of whatever variety, have no *existence* until the artist brings them existence as a sense object of some kind. He puts them into the sensible world. At that point they are factual and no longer have to rely on the 'imaginative construct'. Neither do they, at this point, have any difficulty being truth, and philosophic reasoning persuades that *once* a truth, forever is it so. If a thing comes to pass then, it does so *because* the *possibility* of its true being precedes it.

This encourages us to suppose that in some way it was in some condition of *being*, before the artist put it 'into the sensible world'. It suggests the artist is not, like God, creating out of nothing, but retrieving, for the sensory world, a disembodied entity and giving it sensory form. What the artist makes then, or the composer, for his human witness, is the *form* in sensory terms, of something already real and true if this is the case, however previously unseen. To follow Diodorus and his Master Argument for a moment, it would not be possible for the artist to make *true* something which was impossible, so that this suggests it cannot be that it was *ever* without true being, and was always possible, especially as now once witnessed, and clearly true and physically evident.

As I have said already, it is *possibility* that holds the solution. Possibility of being truth is a superimposed state of pre-existent truth, but not an entity, and is not the same thing without activation as *being* truth. Possible beings of truth are speculative constructs without provenance or required instances as phenomena in the world. It is like there being a vast wall of coat hangars, and it is by will that any of them are made to function as what they are. While what the artist makes may be possible, and may articulate within physics, the sole authority as truth that it has is *subject* to the artists *creative will*. Metaphysical endorsement of what is to be a phenomenon does not diminish in any way the work of the artist. He is, as Balthus declares, dealing with a *divine aspect* of things, a worthy enterprise of value. He is a man of spirit. It is here we find the solution required.

What the artist or composer creates does not in fact pre-exist *independently* as a physical 'thing', but the *possibility* of it however *is* pre-existent as metaphysical truth for it to be realised. It is entailed in the disposition of the creative will with which a given human individual is endowed. Private potential is an aptitude of creative will itself, and also what personalises the work of any artist; he engages with what many have called the 'muse'. What he produces is merely an extension of him, and as he is a true being, what he authorises also is *potentially* truth being, whatever it may be, though he may never activate it. In this case, always it was a potentiality of truth being, dependent always on his will.

The special talent of the artist is the gift of making tangible, by his creative connecting with unseen things to which his will is drawn intuitively, objects of contemplation, that have antecedent metaphysical 'substance', as 'compossibilities' *particular* to his creative will, and that may have no previous sensory manifestation, other than the work at his hands. This bridging, and transcendence, is *a divine skill*. Given his authenticity as an individual, *all the potentialities of his creative will* is the pre-existent being of truth, whatever product or thing emerges from it. Their provenance as beings of truth lies in this creative will. They all have 'delegated' credentials and authenticity.

He is imaginatively endowed even to 'make believe', and to invest truth and reality of counterfeit kind in things he foreknows even to be fictional. At times it is difficult to discern when the artist manifests things of true being, or things of fiction, and this may add further excitement to his activities. His scope is therefore vast and rewarding, both for himself and for the observer. He is capable of sculpting something purporting to *represent* the true being of something, when there is in truth no such thing. The representation he creates however, *is* a being of truth, and *is always* a potential of his creativity. This is a measure of the fluidity of a creative will.

It is said that it is 'impossible for one individual to inspect another's ideas', and this is important in the area of creativity. If an imaginative 'thing', was never to materialise and be made sensible to the world, it could not achieve public 'factual' status where it is sensory truth, like our representation above. However the artist may access an object of being, which he can contemplate, *unless* he gives it sensible form, men may say of it that it is not true, it does not exist, and however intimately he may be acquainted with the true being of such an object, or be enabled to contemplate it, always it must remain private. It is not shared publicly as 'truth'.

This does not affect the object's true being, (of non-sensory variety), and even if always it merely remains only a potentiality of his creative will. But, as we have no other access to each other's objects of contemplation, or to peek into another's creative will, to preview what is possible at another's hands, it is the business of the individual artist to grant *existence*, to his contemplative objects, in the sensible world, where they may become public.

The painter Balthus, who says he paints the 'divine aspect of things', echoes Philo's notion stated earlier of the 'divine articulation in nature and man's intelligence'. Man's creative will is internally related to this. This is engagement with the logos, (the intelligible and 'intelligible to us principle'). Again it is by the intelligibility of an object itself, whether sensory or abstract, and by man's intelligible connection with both, that the artist, novelist, and composer, is the natural *agent of mediation* between sensory and non-sensory, physical and spiritual, natural and supernatural, coexistent realms. What artist or composer is not responsible for spreading his fingertips wide within the deepest and most private cell of the soul?

In view of everything to this point, are we expected, we may wonder, to credit sure and certain truth and reality to ghosts, fairies, unicorns, and Hansel and Gretel, on the grounds that they could not be objects to contemplative acts of thought, be imagined, created, or turn up in books, unless they have true being already? That in fact anything fanciful, however bizarre, is pre-existent and thereby justified by some form of metaphysical *being*, even before we fancy it? The unhesitant answer to this is an emphatic 'no', and for very good reason.

The artist pursues not truth alone, but also predetermined falsehood at times, and for this no *necessary* true being of anything is object to his act of thought, so that the sole authority for what emerges is the dispositions of creative will he owns. He can as easily substitute the false object to contemplate a pink elephant, as he may the true object, (as physically instanced in the world), of a grey one. This is merely the unbounded power of the creative will at work. His fictions, *as spectres of unreality*, are in his arsenal of compossibilities, and, therefore, *as entities of non-true being*, have preauthenticity and credentials where he chooses to exercise his creative will.

Without origination in human will, (a liberty that is self-evident), fictional things like these have no provenance or foundation in anything 'articulating in nature or man's intelligence', such as is applicable to *inferential* problem solving. Instead it is founded solely on an author's will *to image*, and the licence of his creativity.

When it is the case that a predecided point of reference governs the issue, like invention, what is contemplated is predetermined false *being*. Such 'being' is illusion and delusion from the outset. It is essential we make a judgement to avoid indifference between *true* being and *make believe* being. Fictional 'things' displace their falsehood by being the pseudo-intelligible *constructs* of what *imagination* allows. Incredulity is deliberately and intentionally suspended for predetermined purpose. It is quite different for reasoned things of actual true being. These are not constructs or *fabricated*, but discovered by inference reasoning.

Contemplated, remembered, and even imagined things are no more solids than are true being abstractions, but the two are distinct and should not be confused. Both *are* required to be intelligible things, and, it follows, intelligible *to* mind. Both abstract and concrete things, by intelligibility to mind, abide always as supersensory things with no reliance on physics. But whatever lacks necessary provenance are imagined things, having no foundation but the creative imagination, and are predetermined fictions. In their case their authenticity or intelligibility is misrepresented as truth, though they are no more than wilful non-inferential acts of thought.

Other things, of *authentic provenance*, that are not constructs only, cannot be false or fictional. To lack this discernment is a standard feature of a disabled psychology. Remembered imagery referring to objects of thought also may be so distorted or even perverted by admitting feelings or desires.

A logos, or order of intelligibility threading together all true and real things, supporting their own internal order, and the relations between themselves and others, sets the scale of a divine scenario. Man's creative will, imagination, is an archive of potentiality by which previously unseen beings of truth *may* emerge, or alleged and counterfeit *poseurs* of truth may spring. Whether we know the difference and can discern it does not affect in any way the *actual* thread of intelligibility, of infinite, or neoinfinite proportion.

Powerful and creative as man's will may be, it is nothing compared to the greater intelligent forethought and creative will required to grant *him* the exceptional gift of his creative will, and the vast arsenal of potentiality at its fingertips. It is an eternal mind that is evident throughout all creativity and intelligent order, for the outcome thought even alone is self-evident on every hand. Only this is sufficient, or great enough, to meet what is necessary. Only such as this can carry sufficient authorship of the endemic principle of intelligibility that supports both what *lives* and what has true *being*.

In chapters to follow, we continue bridging not *constructs* of wilful imagery, but actuality, of what *is here* with what may be reasoned as *is there*, allowing no intrusive doubt. *We address truth and reality as an endorsement of eternity.*

Chapter 5 – Real here and real there

Intelligibility is what authorises meaning and significance.

At any now moment, in life and experience of the sensory world, when I engage, perceive, or contemplate a face, it is an object of thing about which I will *feel* things. I will feel pleasure, pain, or even indifference, feelings however good or bad, which are familiar to me, and are self-defined objects to my thoughts. Their resonance, as good or bad, is authorised and determined by predilection and disposition, and my attitude will reflect this, often *without* previous life experience, (I may never have seen such a face before, and the infant's untutored smile serves to endorse this). Even before the encounter, I seem familiar very sufficiently with what *to me* is goodness and badness, (whether of faces or other things), inducing me to order my response and attitude, and, just like the infant, with little or no input from life experience required.

Disgust and repulsion seem things for which we need little preparation and which we recognise even on a first encounter with its cause. We are so familiar with the vitalism and *being* of evil and our desire to avoid it, that, when thinking ourselves alone, and tapped on the shoulder, we may be startled, in anticipation of undetermined presenting to us. We are already familiar with a possible scenario from which we know already we would wish to escape.

We may well ask how it is that we should be so prepared for evil or goodness, or indeed many things, whether or not they ever present themselves in life as an actual instance of experience. How is it we are intellectively prepared to apprehend *joy* in the *joyful*, as does our infant, or sorrow for the sorrowful. Even before we experience life instances of these, our psyche is objectively aware of the *intelligibility* and sentiment of *abstract* things, *before* encountering instances of them in the world.

Received wisdom answers this with the notion of *a priori* knowledge, (we know it before we encounter any instance of it), intuitive knowledge, or instinct. I resist exploring definition of these things here in favour of pursuing the different matter that things can be true and real *without* life experience tutoring us in them; that things can be true and real, obtain and prevail, without our having to rely on physics or what is sensory, (for these things leave little room for doubting their verity).

What is more interesting by far is that such things as are *not* self evident by any physical presence, but are abstract, and yet are things with which we are left with no doubt. We have no difficulty distinguishing good and evil as abstractions. *Instances* of them, in the world, 'tune into us' with ease. The instances do *not* precede our insight and preparedness for them. If they did, only then could we say experience is our sole tutor.

Drama too can offer experience we never encounter, yet appeals to us meaningfully even though we know it is fictional. It 'triggers' non-physical things, joy or sadness, (that is very real), that meets the writer's human expectation that his fellows have familiarity with these things. We should remember that much scientific advance is made from the assumption of the truth and reality of something *before* it is verifiable or demonstrated, and not the *other* way about, and this more often explains what we refer to as chance discovery.

Physical encounter of our face as referred to previously seems to render spurious any speculations on its truth and reality, (seeing is believing). But its object to contemplation, as an object to *thought*, is distinctly different in nature. Even a 'remembered' face has no sensory endorsement to support the truth and reality of what we can image within, though we do then know it once existed. When we say 'that's just how I remember him' are we not making reference only to a physical object, however, that *justifies* the *believable* truth and reality of what we now image? For whatever we remember in past time, truly remains in *past* time, and cannot justify our act of thought directed on an object or image now, and *in the present*.

The anomaly here is that habitually for a thing *now* to be true, its authenticity and credibility should, (we feel), be *accredited* to something physical. This is a misunderstanding. Things true *now* do not require physical provenance. The plain ontology of 'truth' is that of an abstraction, a metaphysical property. It is quite distinct from physical 'things', though they may aspire to these also.

Truth qualifies the bonding, unity, and harmony between all authenticates, things party to the whole reality, which is why it is evident in the scrutiny of abstract *or* concrete entities. The dream Parmenides had so long ago indicates that what most clearly concerns issues of existence and life, is opinion, while it is *truth* that substantiates any condition of *being*. It is just as true that beauty *is*, as it is, that an apple *is*. True physical things do not escape this harmony, and the whole of everything composing reality. By motion, endemic to physics, however, there can be changed and evolutionary states of physical things, as motion commands what *is* physical of entities, even where it does not command their true being. This is so up to the ultimate limits of the boundaries of things, (in physics), where they reach a natural point of entropy and rest. A man must grow old and die.

All the changes of motion and physics, to states of affairs, conditions, or things, are no less true than are those things to which they are added. Motion, physics, (as with life and existence), require entities to which they can apply, and these are what we may call 'topmost' or 'prior' entities of *being* status, so that they *may* be *moved* in any way within the zone of physics.

There can be no change, physics, or motion, in anything without the prior *being* of something that *is* to be changed or moved. Physical purchase is only possible where there *is* something. In this way, as Gabriel Marcel supports, we see clearly that life and existence, change and motion, must be added to entities of *being*, things that first *are* something. Growing old and dying are relevant only to physics and life, not the topmost or prior entity of *being* to which these are added.

Every object has associative imagery, but the imagery is not identical to the object. It is a *representation* that implies two things at once. It implies first that something with a basis of truth, (whether concerning physical existing, or abstract being), or associated with a wilful created construct, is *represented*, by imagery. Secondly, images provide substitute sense data, codes in terms of physics, even where an object contemplated may *not* be physical. Imagery is our creative way of doing this.

That my act of thinking is directed at an object as I contemplate it *now* is clearly the case, regardless of imagery, past or otherwise, which *mediates* between my thought and the object *per se*. I may image it as I choose. It follows that the object has independent *being* from my mind, and even the act of thought directed at it, (I mediate when imaging it).

I could not append images past or present, to something known to be true, real, *or* fictional, unless I grant it with all willingness credibility. Mediation is not required unless for some apperception, intuition, or object of imagination, construct, or feeling that the object *is* somewhere. This is so even when I substitute an inventive 'construct' for a true object, suspending my disbelief, as for instance in an illustration, a novel, or play.

If an object we contemplate *was* ever, true, real, and significant, (as in the case of a photograph of my living father), it can never change or stop the *being* of firm identity, (*that* is my father in *this* place, a truth always), regardless of any changes due to physics or entropy, and whether suffered by the father or the photograph. All this amounts to sufficient reason to find such an object, an *objective entity*, credible, and worthy of belief.

However the *truth* 'object' of my father lies beyond capture in terms of physics, for all physical things arrive at entropy. While my father's life is commanded by physics, the always-to-be-true 'being' of him is not. It follows I am obliged to accept that such an entity is inclusive to the metaphysic principle, as a fact, as a pure truth, and that physics has no power to effect change where change is inadmissible.

No 'thing' physical, or degenerative, is self-evidently justified sufficiently to support belief in its unchangeability, but the truth and reality of the *same* object of contemplation is, on the contrary, totally unchangeable. Physics have nothing to do with this, though clearly they underpin the photograph of my father to which I refer, as so also do they in the image of my father made 'permanently', (a qualified description within the limits of its physical deterioration), as *itself* a fixed and unchangeable *sensible* truth.

As I say in the previous paragraph, nothing physical, and this must include the image of my father, and the photograph describing him, can be justified 'self evidently' as an unchanging truth. Yet this seems a paradox if the photo-record is a true facsimile of my father. After all, if a *true* one, as we have seen, it must be unchangeable, and always true, and so it is. How then is it at all possible, we may ask, and with good reason, that a truth that is of sensible identity can be episodic, within the parameters of time, capturing only a 'now' moment of passing time, when the same entity in ten years will bear little resemblance due to inevitable change?

A very pertinent solution offers escape from this apparent paradox. A chameleon may change, though it remains a chameleon, and not a horse. To unveil this I refer again to our boulder as a sensible and intelligible object. As a 'sensible' thing, this is no different to the image of a man in a destructible photograph, for both are subject to the vaguaries and ravages of physics in time and space on the voyage to entropy. Even the sensible truth of the man depicted, in life, is *of* something that must undergo similar change in its physical mode. All these things are sensible and intelligible things, which, in the sensory world, cannot avoid evolving through change. They do not however become something else. There is a crucial element to all these changes that we cannot afford to overlook.

It is not only that all the objects, whether boulder, father, image of father, or photograph, are all intelligible sensible 'things', themselves, and intelligible *to us*, but all their inevitable changes *also*, are intelligible to us. We recognise, and are cognisant of *change* as a built in *property* of physics. In the sensory world, we *know* that boulders can crumble to dust and fathers grow old. The episode of one conditional state is nonetheless no less true and real than the one that follows. In the same way that every card in a pack is a true and real card, no one card constitutes the pack, but is necessary to it. Though cards are shuffled, the pack retains identity. Change does not remove essential identity.

We could have no notion of the meaning or significance of change, the context of physics, without our insight of what it is *not*, changelessness and rest, which is not a property of the sensory physical world, but of what is non-sensory, immaterial, abstract, and in the context of metaphysics.

We each have a grasp, however we choose to ignore it, of the changing and unchanging distinction of two worlds, one populated by physical things, incorporating change, and one by non-physical things, and the unchanging. As we saw earlier *we* must live daily with both tables and trees, *and* truth and beauty. We inhabit coexistent realms. Motion and rest are each intelligible to us and are distinct for this very reason. Both participate in the logos commanding truth, and every human individual is truly here *and* there while in life.

We know that the physical human face, like its physics to which it is a part, is transitory and finite, and is devoid of any means of self supported extension. We know also that we have understandings of such controlling factors as time, quantum, singularity, etc., which would amaze our forbears. In view of this, the lack of durability in a human face, as something spatio temporal, and physical, offers insufficient grounds to convince us that we encounter nothing but an illusion or apparition. The *true being* of something does not require us to witness it. To witness it in addition is reinforcement. There is more than one reasonable argument of support for there being true things we may not witness.

The most common view in support is the social and cultural explanation offered by world faiths, with body and soul, duality, spiritual personhood of some surviving sort through death, the one part of us physical, the other spiritual, one sensory, the other supersensory, durability and survival being assured by transcendence. Applying the metaphysical principle as this does, it cannot be dismissed as the trivial explanation some suppose it to represent. We have seen how abstract entities like beauty are just as true and real as are physical ones.

Another explanation, (not necessarily at variance with that above), is the ancient idea of the *one*, or the Hegelian notion of the *Absolute Idea*, where it is necessary that some whole and sum total of all things is inclusive of everything that can ever be, sensory or supersensory, (and may never be wholly known). This implies ongoingness of some sort like a particular being rested at some terminal singularity, with everything else that is true and real, and where *always* it rests. Again, this does not displace the above, and any scrutiny of the ideas of the *one* or the *absolute* shows they have more in common than in difference.

Yet another and different explanation is offered by Plato, with what is *intelligible*, and a sensory world of physics only justified in its *things* by their origin and derivation drawn from intelligible prototypes, and from which they must proceed. Some convergence of this with the above is possible.

Keeping a grasp on these reasonable notions, though by their nature, theoretical, helps us in reflecting on our encounter with our human face, which, as life experience, is sensory *at* an instant of now, (in some succession of now moments), and *in* a place, so that both time and space are involved. We have seen also that such things of motion, we call physics, are added to something that *is*, and is prior.

A face freshly encountered in life experience, is testament to the physical presence of something in the sensory world; in this case it is a reliable indicator of 'personhood'. As I outlined earlier, all that we need to suppose *further* is that it is a *true and real* presentation of whatever personhood it represents, and what we have looked at already in terms of adding motion to something which already *is* should account for this. In accord with all our preamble to this point, such personhood can never 'cease to be', obliged as it is to be within the domain of the whole sum of things *true* that we may define as 'reality'. Though incomplete because as a particular it is not clearly the *whole* of things, nonetheless it is itself 'real'. It is required for the completeness of the whole. Physical things too cannot exclude themselves from the whole of everything.

Besides this notion of inclusion of our newly met face in the sum total of all things, whether we regard this as the *one*, the *absolute idea*, or alternatively, regard the face as one feature of a *duality*, we have also a true *being* of personhood owning the face. In order for the face to make sense to us it must not only be sensible, but it must also be an *intelligible* object in its many ways, not least of which is so that it may be referred to in speech or thought as a particular attribute distinguishing one of our fellows.

Though the face itself, at some point must decompose after death, the *personhood* it purports is not subject to the same laws of physics, (directed via space-time to entropy as any face is), and, intelligibly *real*, as it is *also* obliged to be, it is clearly further obliged *always to obtain*, though it cannot do this *here* in the 'heimat' of physical laws, *where it has no unending purchase.*

I am at liberty to speak and think of Shakespeare and Napoleon, though now they have no existence within physics; their personhoods are approachable to my act of thinking, in my mind, and thus I apprehend objects of personhood of particular identity. They are intelligible to me, though I have never met them personally, and even if I know nothing of their history as persons, they can still, nonetheless, be 'object' to my act of thinking when once I encounter their names alone, though I cannot 'fill in the blanks', of what personhood they may have had in terms of who they are, or what they did.

Notwithstanding their mystery to me, they cannot help but be clear objects of which my act of thinking has become aware, and if I never become aware of them, their true *being* is unaffected. Once reliably informed of the truth of their erstwhile 'life', they remain objects to my thought, and their *being* is now in addition, *known* to me. If I had not had encounter with them at all, and, now, with their having no physical existence, this does not prevent them from true *being* as objects to contemplation, in spite of the fact that *I* may never contemplate them in person or in sensory ways. Their *being* has no dependence on my doing that, or even on *my* having any awareness of them as persons.

It may be that I come to know of their life and existence by reading or hearing more of them, and this gives the cynic or materialist opportunity to say, well there you are you see, these people are historic and factual, and this is what makes them have any sensible integrity as on object of thought; they are real *because* once they had existence in *life.*

As I believe I have shown, physical life and presence obtains *at a time* and *in a place.* To attribute to a thing truth and reality as *due* to this alone, *where ending and degeneration approaching entropy are inevitable,* contradicts the durability and unchangingness inherent to the intelligibility that endows *being* with meaning. To suggest it is the physical lives of Shakespeare and Napoleon, which have no existence now, is the sole cause for our thought of them now, as *ongoing true beings,* is nonsense. It ignores the fact that unless intelligible beings to start with, and unless intelligible *to us,* (all of which makes them meaningful, true, and fixedly real), they could not *be* an object to thought at all.

What clearly sustains their ongoing truth is intelligibility, intrinsic *to them,* and *making* them intelligible *to us.* Their life and existence alone, (incompleteness without true being), is insufficient without what binds *both* them *and* us. This is not their *physical lives,* but the binding principle of intelligibility authenticating *all* true things. Both Napoleon and Shakespeare, together with our lively thoughts of them, are impossible without intelligibility, and can signify nothing. Reliance on records of physics is a denial of the logos to which all belongs, leading only to the outlook of 'seeing is believing', and absurdity. Without abstractions, as with universals like beauty, no 'thing' is beautiful. Without goodness, there is nothing to which we may aspire. It is intelligence that empowers us.

Even in the unlikely scenario of our forbears inventing such people, to create a colourful history for us, their physical existence may be fabricated, so to please us, but it *cannot* underwrite any true being that they *never* had. Neither could their true being be made false. Again, should we never have heard of either of them, an unerring brute fact remains the case! That we know *nothing* of their lives and existence, or that we know *something* of it, is not at issue. Without intelligible being they are privately meaningless; truth of being for *them,* and truth of being *to us,* and not some spurious register of their birth and death, of which we can be ignorant, is what renders authenticity.

This precisely underpins the authenticity of the countless human beings in the story of the world of which there is no record, but we confidently expect them all to have *true being*. Their lives and existence have no affect on this. Neither does our knowledge or ignorance of them. Within the intelligible principle, unconditionally, they remain inclusive.

What does continue to obtain, then, (when they existed), now, and in future time, and even always, is not their *life*, but their *intelligible being*. It is this that renders significance to them, and not their numbering in the human livestock of a *given time and place*, which satisfies only the sensible and passive intelligibility required of a rock.

To attribute their truth and reality as due to this alone, where it must *end* in degeneration by the motion of physics, (something past and gone), contradicts the ongoing durability that intelligibility requires of what is enduringly, and unchangeably, true and real. To suggest the physical lives of such a two is the sole cause of our thought of them *now*, not only reverses the order of what is added to what, but totally ignores the fact that without the binding thread of the intelligibility principle, providing *awareness and recognition*, both they, *and* our lively thoughts of them, would be impossible, and could signify nothing at all. As a denial of the logos, this is hardly anything but absurd.

With the cynic, we are back to our aforementioned coding and imagery habitually dependent on provenance in terms of physics. I do not have to know of something physical by personal acquaintance, for it to have true life and/or being. He misconstrues my becoming aware of them, my knowledge, as *causing* their having true and real *being*, while it is nothing of the sort. As with grains of sand, I *may* come to know of them, but I may *not*, and such true and real grains of sand as truly there are, will not be affected in either case. All they require to be is intelligible, *as* grains of sand, or as true beings, and not *known as* such.

This is a common misconception. The reality of any thing, is underwritten by its being true, its repletion, completeness, intelligible identity, its durability, and position of rest. This is so whether or not it is *caught up in motion*, as all things of physics are, or whether or not it is known. Instead, true registration as *intelligible* things self-defines what is real. For things such as these there is no time, no motion, and no change. Life and existence apply within physics, a world in flux, where *all* 'things' are in motion, (implying space-time), and all is episodic as it travels to entropy. There is no ongoingness (to existence), for the continued motion excludes any arrested state of affairs, and certainly, in this context, there can be no completion, no point of rest.

The sole way that things of life and existence may claim credentials, to be recognised as 'real', is by their conjoinment, with intelligibility, making them necessary; then are they two in one, sensible *and* intelligible. This is whole and complete *being*, the primary, (or non sensory substance, or spirit), added to the secondary, *life*, in the case of human individuals. Gabriel Marcel as I mentioned earlier puts it that life is a 'gift' added to 'being'. As we have seen earlier, even the inanimate 'object' must be intelligible as such in order either to exist, *or* to be contemplated. Things have no less truth and reality there, as contemplative 'objects', than they do here, as tactile physical ones.

In this vast universe which dwarfs us, and as Russell supported in a previous chapter, we are empowered to stretch our expectations by making inference, all the time knowing that we cannot be aware of everything. At times, things, (or ideas), may present to us without ever our looking for them, and we are then obliged to make some relation to them.

The remarkable Hawking gives us a view of such things that we can never hope to see, such as a universe which may well incorporate beginning and ending. He expands our expectations into such things as points of singularity, where light, gravity and matter, indeed everything, may expand or collapse. Though this enables remarkable things we can *never* encounter, we can see how all things inherent to the universe are dependent upon the mediation of something *intelligible*, itself something we can reasonably infer, and grasp, a something greater and unperceivable, to which all smaller things are a part. Although in this instance we contemplate physics, albeit in some form beyond us, it seems to echo the Hegelian notion of the Absolute.

Even within physics, the notion of a truth and reality harmonizing and binding all things, can readily be appreciated, and yet *see* it we cannot, (something infinitely greater than the many different and separate categories of truths we encounter daily). Something commands and mediates these, not even necessarily a single universe, but there is now even the possibility that what is greater than things, may not be only *our* universe, but many.

We find ourselves, like all else, merely fragments to a whole. We are confronted with something we can never physically observe. In such circumstances, where we cannot even grasp things that *could* be observed, should we for a moment, think it odd, that we cannot grasp any whole understanding of abstract truths that are clearly *unobservable*? Everything is commanded by something vastly greater, *even* in terms of physics. Our freshly encountered face earlier is not so complex, though certainly it is a *required* fragment of whatever *does* command all things, and there is no way even such a particular as our face can be dropped from the scenaric sum of all 'real things', or be ignored.

In the chapter to follow we continue to pursue the particular core of intelligibility informing and infusing all that is concrete and that is abstract, so that both classes of 'things' are unavoidably and forever meaningful; things in motion, in other words, and things at rest. Any narrative of an integral 'whole', if it is to be of substance, implies that *all* its 'particular things', without exception, are *required*.

An unchangeable reality

Chapter 6 – Intelligibility and Truth

What is material must matter while what matters needs not be material.
Both nourish our philosophy of feeling.

Without truth and reality there are no means by which being *anything* can have credentials, authenticity, or provenance. Nothing could have any real identity. There are firm offers of theories procedurally identifying, or verifying, the true being of things, by such as correspondence, coherence, and pragmatism, intended as procedures to identify what is true.

Oddly, it is not what essentially is intelligible sufficiently to present to us as *being*, in the *first* place, that such verification procedures define. What they do define is what is intelligible of them *to us*, (like a study of *what can be known*), and this is what such procedures scrutinize. Whether they should be regarded as wholly definitive of the truth of what presents to us may remain questionable. In spite of their differences, however, what is common to them is the hoped for confirmation of unity, a bonding, between things, revealing some attribute or quality of truth that (it is implied) all things share.

If a thing actually presents itself, (a question we do need to raise to discount illusion), self-evidently it is sufficiently intelligible to be something. As Leibniz would encourage, there must be sufficient reason for this 'thing' to present as something, and this is whether or not we are later able to verify it, and even if we are not. This applies whether to phenomena or noumena, whether things tactile or abstract.

The point I wish to make here is that whatever verification procedure may be undertaken after encountering an idea or thing, (and whatever the result of it), always there is the possibility of doubt remaining, and it should be factored into any ultimate judgement made. It is by the weighing of doubt against certainty that any such judgement may be found sufficiently reliable.

Our mindset, philosophic attitude, private interests, and the strength of intuitive appeal of something to us, may subscribe much to our doubt or certainty, and it is such a matrix as this we may describe as our *philosophy of feeling*. If our doubt of 'ghosts' is strong enough with regard to things of this kind, verification procedures of any quality may be resisted or ignored. Likewise, if our certainty in these ways is powerful enough, any procedure suggesting otherwise is equally likely to be dismissed.

Our *philosophy of feeling* is clearly influential in our outlook at weakest, and our chosen reliable guide at its strongest. We cling or are repelled by encounters of a wide variety, only because they have an imminent intelligibility to us, and it is this that endows them with credentials and authenticity, even in the face of well-reasoned opposition.

What is more important than procedures of verification, is whether things-in-themselves, whether abstractions engaging mind, or tactile things we observe, are intelligible to us by whatever means, intuitively, instinctively, by use of reasoning etc., for if this, they are then self evidently a fragment pertaining to the overall harmony that intelligibility underpins. Applying verification procedures are then unnecessary.

It is not a measurable Truth *outside* the *being* of things, like some attribute and quality or something 'else' beyond them against which they should be measured that should command our attention. It is the 'something' itself towards which our attention should be directed with a view to its intelligible being, and thereby 'truth'. Truth is more intuitively *recognised* than reliably measured. I believe there to be good reason for this, and that it is not to be found in the evasive declaration that truth is that found not to be false, a statement endeavouring to explain something by means of what it cannot be, which is hardly a happy effort. Precisely what this does *not* do is address truth itself, as a threshold of command for anything aspiring to true being.

Truth is 'intuitively recognised' when something independent of sensory experience is intelligible to 'mind' of any variety, concrete or abstract. Whatever presents is a spontaneously objectified, self-evident fragment of what is possible, even where we have no physical experience of any instance of it in the world. Truth binds them all, as things, to *being*, (intuited or experienced), like glue, as various components of reality.

In the case of intuition, no expectation or anticipation of a thing is premeditated. Things require truth in order to *be* at all just as in the sensory world water is required for there to be fish. It bears mental equivalence to the sensory experience of finding a pear in an orchard, or a verb in a sentence. If in the context of our mindset or private interests it feels right, makes sense, and seems at rest we may quickly bind with it.

Of course what appeals in the intuitive way seems to require no questioning. Often however it is convergent with our private interests and predilections, and what we can in life experience, of truth, often marries with what we intuit also. It is a portal of access to truth without the need to apply our senses.

Before ever pursuing the *relations* of things *to* truth, such as things corresponding, or being coherent as having some equivalence with truth, we are obliged to acknowledge that as our starting point, we own a presupposed intuitive belief or knowledge that there is something, of very real *being*, which we describe as 'truth'. We not only regard this position of *presupposing* as entirely reasonable and respectable, that truth *is*, but also rely on it as a dependable springboard for all decisive and intended purpose throughout our living and experiencing. In spite of its abstraction then, and lack of materiality, for 'solid' it is not, clearly truth is 'something' which we cannot reasonably resist or exist without. We are also obliged, not only to exist, but also to exist reasonably.

If all things, statements, propositions, concepts, or material things, including apples and buildings, are nothing unless grounded in truth, truth is clearly *necessary* for anything that is said to be. Further to this, truth does not occur *when* a 'thing' or event occurs, conveniently coming about when a thing does, but the thing or event is nothing unless it *is* of truth. As there is no simultaneity of occurrence between things and truth, (for true 'things must have primary true being), things do not pertain *without* truth, so that things of true being are truth as a matter of course.

What has to be decided about them is their intelligible being as 'things'. It is the intelligibility of things, not truth *per se*, that verification procedures are designed to evaluate. These procedures are open to error that *belief plus justification* usually is not. It is reasonable therefore to conclude that such a belief may therefore have greater persuasiveness than a procedure of analysis. Whether we analyse everything or not, clearly there is a place for faith on encountering things, and as we already know we cannot know everything, it is often in such gaps that we find its place.

As there is no *being* without truth, nothing can come to be true *after* coming into being either, which is clearly impossible. An event coming about in the world is obliged to be in truth a *possibility* to start with. Truth then cannot be other than of *prior* place, before even the first of any things or events can be what it is. In applying verification procedures we are hoping to arrest it. Without truth already on offer, nothing can come to *be*. All must originate and emerge from truth that must precede *anything* coming about. If truth is not primary to the origin or creation of the universe, nothing consequent can 'come to be'.

It should not surprise us that truth remains primary to all considerations since. We can know this to be so from the plain fact that truth is unchangingness, it is unalterable, and always obtains regardless of circumstances. All our procedures of measuring it, convergence, correspondence, etc., would be absurd if it had no *being*. Further to this we know that truth did not occur *after* some lapse of passing time and space, for then time and space would themselves be meaningless, for without truth they cannot *be*. Clearly truth is of metaphysic standing, and a primary abstract elemental.

It follows that truth authorises the *being* of anything, that it is the necessary provenance, inception, and fixed seal of actuality required in the origination and occurrence of anything significant. Without this credential, all is meaningless. No concrete or abstract 'thing' is meaningful without it, and all significant things, propositional or apprehendable, must be *of* it, and fragmentary *to* it. Truth is the complex, the whole, of whatever can be said to have actual *being*. It is clearly foundational and absolute in any consideration of the whole of all that can be, the 'one', or the sigma. It is ultimate harmony.

This bonding and unity of all particulars, in an everlasting truth of reality, can be demonstrated, grasped and understood, by means of theoretical physics, where all is subject to the command of a universe, (or universes), as with our own planet earth. This event leads to another, our personhood, as individual humans, and bound with the earth. We can therefore readily infer that we, and our earth, have common origination in a point of singularity in the cosmos. To do this we ignore the time gap, to see the truth of it. Further to this, the same truth that authorises the possibility of an expanding universe authorises also that of human *being*. To the pragmatism of physics in motion this has temporal efficacy, but to truth it is eternal and unalterable.

Truth is the foundation of all factual *being*, and we, in the context of our universe, are obliged to come to terms with all we contemplate as derivative of truth. Our level of science demonstrates this in physics. We sit truly having tea in our favourite restaurant, only *because* it is true the universe began and continues to expand. Remove truth from the circumstance of origination, including that of our universe, and nothing remains. The universe *is*, and we *are* sipping tea, and it is not time plays *any* part in this, but truth. The universe coming into being, and our sipping tea, are not granted and authorised by time, but are fragments of one 'whole', truth, which never becomes untrue, or changed, and both events obtain *always*, however fragmentary of the whole of truth any particular may be. Had neither the universe nor the human individual manifested, independently truth allowed *always* the possibility of both. This we can *know*.

With truth a primary to all things of real outcome, and with our knowledge gathered of the universe and our situation sipping tea, what we readily recognise of truth is in the outcome of what it authorises. This explains our interest in measuring it by convergence and coherence procedures. It also explains that our living and experiencing as human individuals is *a posteriori*, so that our appreciation of it as *anything* is revealed to us by experience.

Truth by experience of outcome, however, although it is open to empirical judgement and verification procedures, and therefore at best not open to question, is not the sole way that we are aware of truth. But because we apply procedures of verification on a regular basis in the sensory world, it induces a reliance on them that becomes habitual, so that in contrast to their known reliability, truths accessed by other means, such as reasoning, revelation, instinct, or insight, (or justifiable belief or faith), seem by comparison, at least open to question, and even worse, downright unreliable, as they do not seem available to any sort of empirical inquiry. If they were of course, they would not be what they are anyway, as is clear with faith. There would be no need of it.

This does not of itself, however, make these more oblique pathways to truth, (not open to public testing procedures), unworthy of an investment of reflective belief, so long as they are emotively and intellectively sanitised of *delusion and desire*. Though they may not be publicly tested by empirical means, privately they are scrutinised for their validity by significant private interests inwardly contemplated, (intuitively), the degree to which they may be doubted, and to whatever degree we feel it to be an object of awareness, (noumena).

Often these things are identified with *innate* or *a priori* knowledge. Debate continues as to whether these are tendencies of the mind, even unconsciously, towards *necessary* truths. It may help us here to recall that truth itself, as we see above, (though an abstraction), is something we *presuppose* in similar fashion.

That it is in the gift of truth to dispense unlimited possibilities is how it is that all things and events, concrete and tactile, as with physical things, or as seemingly flimsy or abstract, like thoughts and ideas, are by their truth perpetualised as what they are. Time is hopelessly incapable of bringing any sort of change to them. This is why it is said that in the case of any great human tragedy, it is never less a tragedy on the grounds that much time elapses since it occurs. The truth of it is unchangeable. Only circumstances of physics are changeable by time, while the metaphysic principle, encapsulating truth, is beyond physics and beyond time.

There are so many particulars, concrete or abstract, that are nothing without truth, and the intelligibility it dispenses to all of them, (making them all participant to a grand reality), and it is on such a vast scale, a complete understanding of the nature of truth may remain ever opaque to us. We cannot physically observe the origin of the universe, and are condemned only to inference as to what exactly is in ultimate command, but it is clear *something* is, and that the truth that impels all reality is close to it. As intelligibility is inherent to both things and their order, whatever does command carries implication of deliberation and intent, and therefore some boundless variety of *mind*.

In these circumstances, 'God' presents as a reasonable proposition, or, as St Anselm puts it, as the 'best possible solution'. In the same way we cannot observe cosmic singularity at the beginning of time, neither can we identity that thread of truth made explicit by intelligibility, the logos, or sigma, for we do not know all that it includes. In the same way we cannot know every grain of sand on a beach, we cannot know every knot in what may be an infinite rope. As some aspect of eternal mind, all particulars seemingly of purpose and intention, by unity with truth, from the simplicity of plants to the innocence of animals, or even the order of the heavens, hold impressive credentials.

Making our way through the opacity and vastness of what confronts us here, we can be faced with the infinite regression familiar to the quandary of the 'argument of the first cause', or even the slightly different notion of there being an 'unmoved mover', where the 'buck stops', so to speak. This should not however tax us unduly, for we are human, and, as we have seen, cannot hope to know all that can ever be, the whole of reality, as was abundantly demonstrated by our scrutiny of beaches previously. However, with one thing we can rest with some ease, our distinct probability that there *is* some sum total of *all* real things, albeit we can never become acquainted with it, and *whatever* it may include.

Verifying usually follows the course of establishing a model or construct grounded in science, but any ultimate realityscape is both an unknown and an unverifiable thing, so that we are obliged humbly and submissively to 'take it on board' however mysterious. Effective as it may be in practical matters, verification merely persuades or convinces of the truth (of something) that, as we have seen, is prior to it and may be presupposed. From all we have considered so far this is so of a realityscape. It is this then presents the definitive 'unity and bonding' or harmony of all true things.

We cannot however use such an approach with expectation of coming to understand comprehensively the ultimate realityscape, though, like Archimedes earlier, we may freely estimate it. Verification usually follows what previously had been only surmised, but it should be remembered that we can only surmise it if we have good reason to do so by some 'thing', or object, presenting to us to start with. We are obliged to 'objectify' ultimate reality as the 'one', the 'absolute', the whole of everything of truth.

As we found above, the grains of sand on our beaches, actual or metaphorical, are effectively unlimited, so that we cannot hope to find or document each of them. We are left to settle, in this regard, for a principle that all things, whether in space-time or without, are *inclusive* to *all* that can have being, and are required fragments of the whole of everything, and, to echo Parmenides, 'cannot cease to be'. Further to this, what *is not* can have no being, truth, or reality, for *any* thing contemplated, must either be *sensible* or *intelligible*, if it is to be contemplated at all. To be these things, truth must play its part. Though a thing need *not* have sensible presence, it *must* have an *intelligible* one.

To attempt to define truth and reality as anything less than the whole of all that can be, does no more than the anodyne explanation that it is a 'state of affairs', but as I have indicated this may be the best we can do. Russell speaks of it by way of definition with his 'terms' and 'relations' uniting into a 'complex', but this is very much an 'under view' rising to an occasion of unity from particulars of one sort converging with known facts which coalesce into only a 'thing'; details, as we may see a word in a sentence, or a brick in a wall, conforming to a 'larger' something, though still themselves only fragments. That way one can advance no further than some subordinate complex rather than toward some greater 'pan-complex' inclusive of lesser ones. No overview of reality itself is accessible this way.

If we speak of any complex, it should be that of the *wholeness* of all that *can* reasonably, or, better, intelligibly, be, (ultimate harmony and bonding, the one, the absolute), rather than incomplete and fragmentary complexes, for without truth and reality in toto, *nothing* can claim any *required* reality. The reality we consider can be no less than the complex constituted of all *true* things.

Reality then is best approximated as an uninterrupted perpetuity of all that is true, at a position of rest, so that any proposition that explains reality in terms of physics and material *things in motion* is hopelessly insufficient and absurd. Reality is very clearly a deficient complex without required intelligible abstractions, such as goodness and triangles, which, though not physical, are yet undeniably *truths* that cannot end. Physical things are truths that can *physically* end, but as truths, are obliged *always* to obtain. The result of this is that we are obliged to recognise that it is only the physics that ends. It follows that in our consideration of true physical 'things', their 'truth' is unalterable and extended. What is material must matter, *in passing* to physics, but *always* to metaphysics. Without the matter of bodies we cannot *exist*, but without what matters truly *besides* them, we cannot *be* anything.

Commonly we acknowledge the world to be full of sensible and identifiable 'things', including human personality and private disposition. When no longer they can be sensed, *in* a time and *at* a place, (because sensible things *must* be sensed), we can rightly say they are not *here*. When we say they no longer *exist*, this too is an undeniable fact; a fact however, of the business of life experience, where we must engage with space-time and physics, where things can become worn out, expire, be demolished, and are no longer physically present. While that is all well and good, it has no affect whatsoever on their *true being*. Physics is irrelevant to that, and we enter what is governed *beyond* them, within the metaphysic principle.

We may rightly feel some of these passing things of physics are sadly missed, and even grieve for them, but what we grieve for are in a sensible world where nothing lasts, for all things must be in a state of change under the principle of physics. Here, all things obey the law of wear and tear and passing successive time, whether instants or episodes, the very things that epitomize what are 'sensible' within time.

It is now we should ask ourselves what it is that makes these 'things', including human individuals, at all coherent and significant to us, and, we are obliged to assent that this is due to distinct identity, not in some sensible variety, which is only absurd, but in the meaningful way that these 'things' are *intelligible objects*, to which our act of thinking can be directed, and where they are not solids, we must acknowledge they are nonetheless *truths* 'objectified'. We must grieve for our fathers and those who pass the way of physics. They are objects of contemplation to our act of thinking *because* they have *true being*, but this is no variety of physics. What, we may ask, can carry their identity, with particular attributes and qualities? How do they objectify?

There is no significance or meaning to them unless, besides being an apple or a person, in sensible substance, things are not *also* recognizable as an *intelligible* entity with alternative substance *other* than sensible. To be sensible and unintelligible is impossible. To be intelligible a thing must be a truth. After all, it is *because* they are intelligible that we can freely speak meaningfully of them, and think of them, at *all* times, and whether or not they *exist* 'here', in the sensible world, and regardless of the fact that we cannot *see* them 'here' any more. This is the way of 'objectification' that we are obliged to adopt. Clearly 'things' are capable of transcendence, always presenting as 'objects' on the basis that they are *intelligible truths*, and more than passing sensible objects.

This suggests, as do Plato or Aristotle, that whether or not they have sensible substance, their identity must have *other* substance, or essence, which is *not* sensible. This substance or essence is the *being*, incorporate to truth that already we have considered, and to which it is a fragment. Clearly *the intelligibility of things is the linking thread to truth that is unchangeable*, the 'logos', or Plotinus' 'chain of being', the metaphysic principle.

Applying the Russell logic from the opening of my Introduction, because we cannot see such and such a substance, which is non-physical, does not show it is not there. Though we may have no experience of the non-physical entity, like ghosts, in life, or in the sensible world, (and like the dark side of the moon), we yet remain justified to speak and think of them as objects of contemplation, (by means of their intelligibility). We do so therefore in *anticipation* of their reality, as with the dark side of the moon. This is often intuitively so, even where we cannot *experience or see* precisely what we contemplate. Things require only to be intelligible to be incorporate to truth. This is so whether there are instances of them within physics and the world or not. Though we may merely come to know of a physical thing once extant, and now no longer in sensible form, by intelligible form, though clearly not *here*, always it remains an unchanging truth, and must nonetheless, be *there* for us to contemplate it.

This notion is further reinforced by the fact that, whether we are party to a single universe, or a complex of them, and whatever the whole truth and reality may in sum total be, and even though we cannot model this, every detail and particular of that whole truth complex is a required component of it. Its sum total requires each and every component to be accountable in order for bonding and unity to occur. This is our total harmony of a position of rest. This suggests a particular intimate relation between any physical substance to which qualities are attached, and its non-physical counterpart, engaged by thought, and a *true* object.

In addition to this, in view of the need for a sensible thing also to be an intelligible one, (otherwise it could carry no identity), that any thing may endure, by being 'sensible' alone, is insufficient. It is an incomplete condition omitting uninterrupted intelligibility, which is *additionally required* for it to qualify as true, and also as any sort of significant feature of the whole, 'realityscape'.

Synthesising advances made over centuries of philosophic insight, I am persuaded that it is only reasonable to conclude that no sensible thing, including human personality, can exist in life and engage with experience, in the sensory world, without its intelligible credentials, which themselves confer and authenticate meaning upon sensible form. It is these compose the 'truth object', the unchanging identity. The force of this is demonstrated clearly by the fact that it is not the vehicle of the personality, the body in the case of a human individual, the material and the flesh, but the intelligible being that is the *truth* of it, that is in any way capable of linking with thought as an intelligible object.

The sensible object may be the body, while living, but the 'always' true-being is the truth-object authorising it.

Whether ultimately all this is so by some commanding complex of universes, or God, any *form*, identifiable in sensible context, and therefore *also* as an intelligible entity, has no choice but to be party to the sum of all things true and real. Forever must this be, beyond any strictures of time to which sundry sense objects alone are exposed. Plato takes this much further making intelligibility from where all things originate or derive. The mystic aspect of this discourages the notion that sensible objects are to be inclusive to the *whole*, the sense object *plus* intelligible object, and departs from any reality *in Toto*, inclusive of *everything*, and that is more my direction here.

As the sensible object must also be intelligible to speak and think of it, the sense object must be whole in itself, (as sensory *and* non sensory), and a required fragment to what is whole of reality. It is impossible for it only to be sensible. Intelligible and true, it cannot merely be a sense-object. Neither can it be erased. My own persuasion more lies at the core of the work of Parmenides, where anything that truly *is*, cannot, ever, *cease to be*, though it may certainly cease to *exist*, a quite different thing, for its intelligibility remains, as exemplified by revisiting an object of sense in any way, (as by memory or depiction).

A thing is intelligible *by* its intellective appeal as a bounded entity, self standing, and clearly defined; not by any coherence it can have as a corruptible object, subject to change, for that alone, as we see, is always decidedly incomplete. To have any claim to reality it must be also intelligible, (make sense). The act of perceiving, (perception), indicates the entity of an apple, as a physical or sensible 'thing', but it is an act of thinking, (conception), confirms the truth and intelligibility of the apple, and thereby its completeness as a *true* entity.

This is where illusion often finds purchase, where confirmation by intelligibility is withheld. The sensible nature of our apple is corruptible, by time and change, but its intelligibility remains unaffected, for this is not commanded by time. It follows that the object to sense, (whether an apple or our father), is corruptible by time, as is the *life* and *existence* of all sensory things, but the intelligibility of them, as 'true things', and of reality, is not. What is significant concerns not their life and existence, but their true *being*.

Clearly it follows that the *life and existence* of a thing is best conceived as effectively conducting itself like a property of, (or an addition to), intelligible *being*, (the essence or substance of something of truth, and which is *not* sensory). This 'two in one' identity is a particular reality and truth as it pertains to a sensible object. As we have seen, it could not be at all without its truth and intelligibility. Endorsement and affirmation of the sense object is provided by that to which it is allied, and it is *this* can be revisited, reviewed, researched, and, *in life*, reconsidered, or contemplated. This is so whether we focus on an apple or a human individual. Both are fragments of truth.

It should be noted here that in no way does this reasoning justify any theological proposition that an apple may have a soul, for we engage here with only factual elements of truth, in demonstrating any perpetuity for an inanimate and passive sense object. No inanimate object without the active capacity of self will, can carry self-responsibility. Though an apple may qualify as an intelligible truth-object, and it is therefore intelligible to us, nothing is intelligible to an apple.

A sense object may be engaged *after* its life or existence, for example, as an object of memory, dream, or depiction. It is, in fact, always, (once intelligible, a true *being* of valid origination), both of sensory *and* intelligible significance, and beyond the corruptibility of any sense object indicated alone by sense, (which could only be illusory).

In general, we must come to terms with grasping in what state of mind we capture a decided understanding of a given physical object of *thing*, or its metaphysic counterpart as object of *thought*. Whichever it is we engage with as an object of either kind, it involves *mindset*. This in turn will employ *retrospection* or *introspection*.

It is by some given mindset that we dispose ourselves towards encounter of either *things* or *thoughts*. This disposition may be predilective, based on what 'goes before' the 'now' moment, and therefore retrospective, or it may be based on things or thoughts that present with 'immediacy' now to our contemplation of them, which is introspective. If we find some predisposed *attitude of mind* must be disposed of in favour of another more persuasive one, then we have explanation of the human capacity for the *changing of mind*, where the consequence is one of altering viewpoint by a mind.

If however we have sentiment and preference for clinging to the physical object, as it *existed* in *past* space and time, and to maintain the *retrospective mindset* that accompanied it, this desire is obliged to inhibit *introspection*, and we will avoid what challenges our desire. This is a common obstruction to advancing to self-resolution and orientation with any suggested or more persuasive reality that may be noncompliant with what we desire. This is the position of the materialist when he dismisses the metaphysic principle. He will not compass it.

We must take into account both *what* we recollect, (and even image), *and* our mindset when first we encountered it. These may not concur with our present state of mind towards a thing, and then, in addition, we have the fact that if what is contemplated is something experienced in life and physics anyway, *that* aspect of it *must end*, while the object of thought to which it is now appended always persists. What may be subject to a change of mind, parodied by 'that's all in the past', or 'I can see it now', is a wilfully responsible adopted attitude of dismissal in the first case, or recognition of significance in the second. What it is *not* is any definitive analysis of truth or reality.

Our creative will is therefore a determinant factor in what we are prepared to recognise as a coherent reality, and this is what this book attempts, entirely without any rejecting mindset towards the metaphysic principle, for this evolves from one that is dismissive of the rigid materialist's view that reality is composed only of material *things*. I am persuaded that the true being of *any* thing, including personhood, does not depend on physics, and that nothing is ever *lost* to a realityscape of *truth*.

Ryle's distinction between *retrospection*, or memory, like this, and *introspection*, (inner appraisal made within private minds by acts of thinking directed at objects of contemplation), differs from my own. His distinction proscribes and condemns the eternality of true being to which I subscribe, and is simply not there to empower him to reach conclusions similar to my own. His private interests and philosophic attitude exclude eternality of true being, and he cannot reach out to the extensive being of objects or entities of abstraction, on the basis of their truth *beyond* material things.

Both the *sense object* and its intelligible correlate, (*the object contemplated*), are *each* accessible, however differently, and at any time of our choosing. This is so even whether it is introspection or retrospection that is employed at any given time. The duality of a given identity of *thing* is not a dual identity, but *one* identity of fused relation and alignment. It is the *living* and the *being* of a single identity, whether animate or inanimate.

After life and existence, things once perceived as sensible 'things', may be revisited by image referral techniques, (e.g. what is painted, sculptured, photographed, even thought, and extensively continuing their appeal to sense). On the other hand, they may present as intelligible object of contemplation only, by act of thinking alone, with no ongoing presence as phenomena, (e.g. object of thought by dream or reflection, or even eidetic imagery). This is so for two good reasons; they are of truth and intelligibility.

In view of such connected thought, reliably, hopes and expectations are raised that whatever may be considered *real* 'here', simultaneously obtains always as *real* 'there', by its intelligible credentials and authentic 'shadow'. We are at liberty to think of this as the fusion of mind and body, (two simultaneous locations), for which our duality equips us, to deal with a two dimensional journey among essential *things*, encountering necessary *thoughts*. Both are obligatory and demand our attention, but it must be remembered that what makes them independent dimensions, is also what makes them distinctive, (through conjoined by a singularity of identity), and it is to this now I turn.

When we speak of heaven and earth, the sensible and the intelligible, the sensory and the supersensory, we exaggerate *distinction* between what appeals to sense, and what appeals to thought. Life and afterlife is another such exaggeration. While life and physical experience pertains, we engage with the earth, the sensible, the sensory, but this does not exclude our *simultaneous* encounter with heaven, the intelligible, and the supersensory. That many will deny this does not alter the truth of it.

We do not have to observe by sight what the principle of intelligibility clearly 'objectifies'. Truth, goodness, God, and whiteness, are objectified routinely this way in order to be contemplated and accessed by thought. Such things have presupposed basis of predilective reasoning to them, so that while there may be little direct instance of them in the world, there are indicators or semiotics that clearly imply them. This is not so for fairies and dragons. For *them* to be intelligible objects of contemplation, they must have special licence by the creative will, so we willingly suspend our disbelief of their having any place in truth.

Predilectively we know them to be fabricated 'objects' of no true significance.

Imaginary things cannot be objectified without deliberate projection by the will, but this is not required for truth, goodness, God, or whiteness, which have no reliance on invention. Such things as these are free standing and require no conjuring act. As the saying goes, 'there's no such thing as an atheist in a foxhole', and though it takes certain courage, we may admit to believing in ghosts. This makes both objectified contemplative objects respectively no less than distinct possibilities. No application of any creative will employed is responsible for them.

It is by the same reasoning that the inanimate sense object, such as a material boulder, is potentially a sensible, and frequently 'objectified' thing. Without its truth and intelligibility as the thing-which-it-is, either we suffer illusion, or we believe in a thing wholly based on the sense data we actually receive, which, alone, is insufficient, for without it making *intelligible* sense also, and its inclusion in truth, it cannot *be* a boulder at all. A cardboard or Oldenburg sculpture is not a boulder.

When a cloud presents itself as a map of Britain, *without* intelligibility qualifying and distinguishing the two, we might well take the cloud to be a map of Britain in the sky. It could, indeed, be anything, for alone it is incomplete. Intelligible, it is identifiable, but only sufficiently as a cloud. Truth is as ascertained. We have much support with such a view from the clear observation that *meaning* is implied *by*, relevant *to*, consequent *of*, (and likely entailed *by*), intelligibility, (Philo's divine articulation, the 'logos'), and that without this, all is meaningless, clouds, boulders, or universals.

Intelligibility fulfils two functions in this way. It underwrites the *true being* of a thing of clearly presented identity, and it empowers mind to access the being of things, (by acts of thought), which cannot always be seen by some sensory means. This again is Philo's *articulation* at work. What we access in this way may not be manifest at all in any physical way, but this does nothing to discredit the capacity our empowerment bestows upon us to grasp the unseen by ascertaining it as truly *being*, albeit our senses detect nothing. It must however qualify for this by well-supported and justified presence as a thing *intelligible*. This may be by sensory *or* reasoned procedures, and it must be intelligibly informed and determined, whether or not it is to become 'known'.

How then we choose to model things for ourselves will depend upon our private interests, whether these are essentially sensory or supersensory, or perhaps sensible or intelligible, or even the tactile and the abstract. The fact remains that we can acknowledge the truth and reality of a thing when its presence is wedded to intelligibility as a meaningful 'form', even of either kind alone, for its underwriting as 'truth' is, then, unchangeable, for it is always to be beyond the spatial and temporal.

The only true conflict between philosophers at core lies not with language, as some assert, and confusions arising from it, as others highlight, and not necessarily even in the opposition of self-consistent theories, or in the built-in confusion of semantic debate, as Wittgenstein insists. It lies instead in those restless inner private objects of interest that often philosophers present with dignified coherence, infused with the passionate intensity of a devoted heart, and even where they have no ultimate and objective guarantee of correctness.

They are not disingenuous in this, but modelling the world under the guidance of what it is to which they are wholly devoted. Stoics demonstrate their devotion to inner tranquillity, Christian philosophers their devotion to God. All see their devoted journeys as pathways to the all-governing truth where all histories ultimately must in origination finally and inevitably reach 'singularity'. This singularity is where all word, thought and action assemble as the 'breath of the cosmos'.

What certainly we cannot do is dismiss the metaphysic principle I touch on here, any more than we can ignore what our senses choose to deliver to us, and this raises a two worlds theory. This sure and certain level of equivalence of gravitas represents serious challenge to all but a straw hat. What makes us worthy while at rest with ourselves is total devotion of both our life and our being to what truly we *see*, and, unhampered by our senses, truly *ascertain*; of two worlds; of what here is seen, and what there is ascertained. This is the all-inclusive 'heimat' and unity with reality.

So far I have claimed the permanence, the perpetuity, of whatever is true and real, whether it be an object of thing, a sensible object, or, an object of thought, which may or may not associate with a sense object. Often it is the object of thought, twinned in *life*, with a sensible object, (which extends *beyond* life experience), so that divine aspects of things are attainable. Objectified abstractions like number or universals have no sensible pedigree found in the physical world. They are of another order.

The materialist will suggest of course that numbers are 'logical fictions' and universals would have no purchase without the particulars that give rise to them, but as we have seen, if, like dragons, numbers were products of wilful invention, and merely *fictions*, they could not simultaneously be *truth*. This appears contradicted by the outcome of their manipulation.

In the same breath, he is obliged to concede more interestingly that there is an *eternal* aspect to numbers, (not to mention physical consequences). In addition to this, though we can have no sensory experience in the world *encapsulating* whiteness, it is nonetheless *as* intelligible to 'mind' as is any particular object that may be white, and a man blind from birth can compass it, as in practice I have found. Only faith in an all-embracing truth is required, to speak of things meaningfully, even without experiential 'reconnaissance' in a world of particular 'things'. I hope to consolidate this in what follows.

Chapter 7 – Binding the Sensible with the Intelligible

Furniture is not there only when it can be seen.
Nothing can exist unless also it is a being of truth.

A boulder, a ship, a building, is a 'thing' which is spatio temporal, and well bounded by physics, and, alone, must present only *shifting* identity, for it can neither be permanent, infinite, or ongoing, and in accordance with the physics to which it is bound, be it weather, the hand of man, or even Stephen Hawking's 'arrow of time' in cosmic terms, it must *change* and be transformed in various ways. A boy may become an old man, only, and exclusively, at the hand of physics. Without physics there could be no *change* and no time. Only a boy with no true being, like Peter Pan, could never grow old.

Under the principle of intelligibility, and not to speak imprecisely, there is a way that a boy is never complete, just as he is incomplete as an old man. As a true being and entity of significance, always he is beyond any reach of physics, for both boy and old man are *one and the same* true *being.* On the other hand, the living body is not common in all respects to each case, due to changes. What is altogether intelligible of a boy is not *what proceeds* to being a man at the hands of motion and physics, for his physics are merely the vehicle of physical transition, an intelligible *but* sensible object, a body, that must change, and like furniture, it wears out. The growth of an individuals experience and knowledge demonstrates a feature of this.

This has no affect at all on the being of truth that informs and directs it, and is unalterable. The old man certainly is intelligible as 'old man', but as a sensible 'thing', (or he could not truly exist). At the same time, as such, he is corruptible by change to such an extent that he may be unrecognisable from the boy once he was. This is merely because physics in motion, to entropy, has effected change, through time, of those of his properties *vulnerable* to change. Boys do not grow beards without an input from physics, and time is again needed to make them 'old men'. Physical properties are thus added to the *same* essential entity of being, but are observable only where they have purchase, and that is within physics.

As I have already indicated it is not the intelligibility of necessary personhood, his 'essence' or substance that must move with time, (due to subjection to physics), but the physical attributes and qualities of his person in *life and existence.* Life and existence offers intelligibility as a sense object indivisible from the truth of his being, which is what dispenses authenticity to *presence* as boy *or* man, making *both* intelligible *on account of* true *being.*

Neither boy nor man in life, the sensory world, could he be, if it were not that both are intelligible to us, one single identity under the control of physics where they reach, underwriting stages of change. In the same way, as we have seen, each episode of the one, that is boy or man, are what is significant of one true being, and it follows that it is the boy or man under the command of physics *only* that must encounter end in death. This does not affect the truth of him, his intelligible *being* which is not physical. No physical episode interrupts this, for it is not a physical 'thing', though while such an individual *lives* and *exists, also* he is a sensible human form. Only *this* is subject to physical laws.

The convergence of boy *and* man as *one* coherent identity then, is not some substance or essence that is at all a captive of physics, time, and space, but a 'two in one' complex, in much the same way that a man having consumed an animal becomes two in one. He is an intelligible, and *necessary,* entity, not of sensible life alone, but of *truth-being* significance also. The 'truth-beings' of Napoleon or Socrates have intelligible and essential perpetuity, while this is certainly not so for the vitalism and experience of their *lives,* no longer obtaining in present times. It is not their physical 'bottoms on seats' we continue to admire or regard, but their *truth of being* and personhood, which is impossible geophysically to locate as there is nothing geophysical about this any more.

Comment by J B Priestley on how best we capture the truth, and spirit of this understanding, is worthy of repetition here, for not only is it most apt to what I claim, but it is also something any one of us can experience. 'When a boy looks into a mirror', he says, 'he sees a boy and something else. When he is a man, he sees a man, and something else. As an old man, he sees an old man, and something else'. Priestley puts my case in a most enigmatic and effective way.

In any one of the varieties of episodic physical forms, of sensible 'things' as they proceed to entropy, we may encounter some passing stage of one thing, though the truth of it, and at every stage, retains singular identity, (the boulder as dust, the building as rubble, the young man and the old man). Always we describe them in temporal context. It is not their being, as fragments of truth, but their phenomena emitting sense data we describe.

A train may stop at Liverpool, Crewe, and London. It cannot be in London while it is in Crewe, because it is a train given to motion and existing in one place at a given time. Nevertheless, it is unarguable that the train at Liverpool, Crewe, and London is truth, and *in each case*, and always it remains truth that it is the *same* significant train *at each* place. Physics lends us those tools of description. The descriptions merely accord to given stages of motion and *change by time*. This is merely *spatiotemporal* identity, though not *substantive* identity, and there is therefore no difficulty describing it, (location in space-time of singular entity), at *any* physical stage. The boy and the old man are locked into the same form of existence where change is endemic.

Substantive identity is the 'itness in truth', always at rest, while spatiotemporal identity is the geophysical 'itness of time and place' that *temporally*, a given identity may requisition in the ergodynamic of physics, and motion. All 'things' of relation to an entity are truth, and *as* fragments of truth are *unchangeable*, however any of them are spontaneous as of temporal assignment, so their physical manifestation changes or ends. In terms of truth they are eternal in register.

Stages of temporal assignment also *each* true, are, thereby, manifestation of particular attributes of a given essential identity that we choose to contemplate. We may say, for example, these particles composed a rock, and the rock formed from lava. We have expectation of physics *changing* the state or arrangement of 'things' as they may be observed. It does *not* change the *truth* of the particles, the rock, or the lava, that the object of our thought, that may be the rock. The truth of particles, rock and lava, forever must be so independently of the essential entity we contemplate, and to which change is a presupposed condition. They are valid fragments or attachments to the one and same substantial truth we contemplate. In this case, physics dictate descriptive terms, and this poses us with no great difficulty.

We can describe precisely any object in the context of its timescape, even where composed of differing elements. In the case of our boy and old man we have like substantial equivalence, (or essence of being), with differing presentation. We are habitual in dealing with motion and change in physics, and have descriptions available for periodic change.

We have practically no ways of dealing with the total absence of physics and change, to which our life and experience accustoms us, when we contemplate *unchangingness and rest* such as confronts us with *being*. Consequently we are in the habit of expecting to be capable of *observing* anything that *can be*, for our most convenient tools are well suited to the sensory world of physics.

It is not possible in the same way to describe true *being*, something that must be inferred and indescribable, and without physical definition. We can point to neither place nor time. We have no tools for such a description. There are no such things as motion or change, (time), or space, to compass it, nothing concerned with physics, no constant change and motion impels it, and such things as 'shape' are not appropriate.

Whether encountered as building or rubble, or as boy, a 'thing', in physical terms, is obliged to have intelligible *being* if it is to be of meaningful substance at all, and *however* it presents. Its truth substance, or essence, is only ascertained, accessed, or determined, *in spite of* vaguaries of physics. *That* man is *this* boy, or, this is what's left of the building, is a relational description of one particular substantial entity, (only accessible to thought). Its perpetual *being*, its essence, is distinct from the conditions of its physical differences or distinctions.

In constant shift, as a physical thing, and subject to constant change, in its intelligible *substance*, or essence, it is of unchangeable *meaning*. It may be likened to the fact that a boy, a husband, a father, and a grandfather, due to changes in the world of motion and senses, differing modes at different points in time, differing purpose, (albeit each intelligible), all amount to one thing that *exists* as variously observed. All the physical states bear equivalence to *one* individual, and one *necessary* being. Many socks, shirts, and thoughts, are single owned.

Such a *substance* or essence, of truth, certainly nothing material, may be an object to thought, but not to touch. We cannot hope to observe it. Nonetheless, it is this, (the essential *being* of a thing as truth), which authorises and makes credible any sensory form or identity we encounter. It is the intelligible 'truth-infusion' of sensible 'things' that renders *them* of any significance. Such an infusion renders clear the *meaning* of things *manifested*, however changeable their outer appearance. Without intelligible basis, (meaning), no object of thing is 'readable' in *any* 'form'. However the human individual presents in physical form, as boy or man, he is always the *one* 'intelligible' substance or essence, which time or space *cannot* alter, however it is empowered to manipulate his *physical* form, or even erase it.

We may say the same of any truly significant event. An event may be defined as an instance of life experience, and therefore something very much of conscious register about which knowledge may be gained. All physical phenomena are 'knowable', though they do not *require* to be known. It occurs *at* a time and *in* a space, and must therefore hold sensory significance. But, again, unless intelligible, it could not even achieve that. It is obliged to hold meaning of some order if it is at all significant.

It's meaning *at* a time or *in* a place applies ongoingly and always. It rests with truth. The conscious life experience of an event passes and ends, for it is bound to the laws of physics. The *meaning* it holds, however, as true and intelligible, cannot ever change *or* end. Hence the tragedy that is always so.

Without being *intelligible*, then whatever a thing's attributes or qualities may be thought to be, (as with illusions), no sense can be made of it, and there can be no sense data from it that can be read meaningfully. Precisely the same applies to any given human individual who experiences *form* in the world as a recognisable human individual. It is meaning, (intelligible *substance*, or essence), which infuses him as a 'thing' of truth and reality, nothing corporeal or material, in any spatiotemporal way.

Clearly then it is the intelligibility of a 'thing' which underwrites its meaning and coherence, and whether in the physical form it may be recognised, as in *perceiving* it, or as the object of contemplation to any act of thought, authorising the *conceiving* of it. All that truly distinguishes the *perceived* from the *conceived* is the natural and necessary, (in the sensory world), *instability* of sensible objects, (boulder or person), and the equally necessary ongoing *stability* of the (albeit) amorphous, but intelligible, *object.*

Such a durable and ongoing stable and clear identity, regardless of any metamorphosis, can only best be explained by means of a special relation between attributes and qualities, on the one hand, and substance, on the other. Intelligible *substance,* (or essence, as Aristotle prefers), may best be demonstrated in a way favoured by 'Julia' or 'Julian' of Norwich, and which here I develop.

Taking a ball of clay in the palm of the hand, it has intelligible *substance* as that ball of clay, and is not to be confused with some solid thing with core or pit of a physical nature at its centre, of which there should be nothing anyway. It has meaning and is intelligible nonetheless. Here, even, as object to thought we may *contemplate* it, without having an *actual* ball of clay. We may however knead it, and shape it into many things, a head, a banana, or an animal, all of which are distinguishable and different things to the previous ball of clay.

These differences, (to the ball of clay), by way of animals having tails, and heads having noses, are distinguishing characteristics of identity, but every one of them would be impossible to fashion both without the initial ball of material clay, or, without their integrity derived of making sense, and having independent *meaning*, as intelligible 'things'. That they resemble and refer to things of which there are earthly instances is not the issue, (though it is why we recognise the animals made), but without the clay, which no longer they resemble, they would not be anything.

Animals of physical properties identifying them as sensible objects is potentiality and possibility without ever emerging from the clay. The clay presupplies the truth of them. It is the clay makes them possible. As Diodorus teaches us, what is impossible is not within the gift of truth to dispense. It is in such a way that all things that *exist* emerge from truth. Intelligible *existing* or intelligible *being* originate only in truth where they share authorship and provenance.

Each 'thing' we make, having the credentials and authenticity of individual things, (within space and time), and identity of their own, once were wholly unseen, and merely potentialities, within one ball of clay. Always they are things of truth, *before, during, and after*, manifestation as sensible object. They can even be contemplated before ever emerging, they can be *seen* when they *have* emerged, and they can still be objects to thought even if crushed and returned to the clay ball. This quality of inherent truth of *things* is unalterable.

All throughout their transitional states, whether seen or unseen, all things are emergent, and are intelligible, and thereby *essential* objects, *always*, (even *before* they were fashioned in our example above from the clay, and by the act of thought of a potter). While their intelligibility *always* obtains, at any stage of their presenting to us, they are thus meaningful, at *all* times, but only when the tactile properties of physics are added to them can they be intelligible *sensible* things, and in that presentation, only for a while. Their essential substance, (Aristotle's essence of being), is an intelligible entity, albeit an abstraction, of truth, whether or not physics adds to them.

What connects *all* things is intelligibility, and this articulates as mediator through all that is identifiable, like the rope running through a series of knots. Everything has this 'connectedness' articulating it. This is so on a broad scale when we consider the abstractions of intelligibility itself, where many autonomous and independent minds coalesce in occasions of shared apprehension, as with encounter with universals, not unlike our knots. Though 'whiteness' is something distinctive to each mind, there is agreed recognition of an idea. The 'end idea' is intelligible to many different minds, resembling some point of singularity to which they are indeed 'connected'.

This is as impressive a harmony as is the cosmos, with its variety of individual things or events reducing *in physics* to a point of *singularity* we call the 'big bang', connecting them all. What must caution us here is that the terms of physics channel our thoughts to the 'big bang' as a 'beginning', because physics requires to be understood in its *own* terms of events and 'things' *in motion.* Motion before the 'big bang' is opaque to physics, so we have what we conceive as a beginning of time.

In truth there is no way of certainty that the 'big bang' is really a 'beginning' at all, at least in the way that physics suggest. We have no sure knowledge, for example, that the 'big bang' is not itself no more than a party to some greater 'series'. Nonetheless, the notion can present, only because there are intelligent minds to which such a notion *may* present as intelligible. A thought 'object' of this sort is not derived of physics, but of a mind that is not under the rigid hand of its laws. *Mental life* is not confined, (as neurophysics may like it to be), to the dictat of brain activity, as exemplified in the untutored inexperienced smile of the infant.

Physics is in fact a tool manipulated by intelligibility of the greater order connecting everything, the order rational and intellective, and clearly not the product of any brain that is itself emergent from physics and biology. This is where 'physics as mediator' of any kind becomes insufficient, and must play 'second fiddle' to a greater, more extensive realm of plausibility, so that we find the true mediator is in fact, not physics, but *intelligibility*, intellective power sufficient to authorise the very schema of physics, (for it is one), and this is clearly in the command area of what is beyond them, *metaphysics*.

It is when we engage with physics we speak in terms of *beginning and ending*. in the case of the universe we make use of physics *as if* it were the mediator providing 'links' and supports that we then readily grasp, extending to a point of singularity apprehendable *through* the very same physics that underwrites it. Yet the order observable in this is neither an attribute nor intellective potential of physics. All very material and neat as this may be, it is a 'horse that cannot run'. We are tempted always to rely on what we can observe, in spite of our awareness that there are true things that are unobservable.

It is more reliable to conclude that intelligibility precedes all that evolves, (including physics), and all that has any *potential* to evolve. It gives some kind of 'divine articulation' to everything, (Philo's expression), or everything of truth, including human intelligence. This is what we have in mind speaking of the logos. Clearly it is the same *mediation* informs what is thought and what is manifest, what is concrete and what is abstract, what is imagined and what is made. Always there is this 'connectedness' that bespeaks intellective deliberation in the way it articulates.

In making our heads, bananas, and animals earlier, each of singular identity, we have fixed identity for them by the particular qualities and attributes we attach to each. Although all these are material, and of sensory detection, and therefore physical, there is no physical *substance* to each of them, to which *attributes* are attached. We cannot claim it is the clay, for this, as implied above, is itself derivative of the intelligible archive of *all things*, and not self-standing. We know it is not self-originating. The substance is not the clay, nor the instances of animals extant in the sensory world.

The true substance of the animals we 'make' clearly cannot be physical. It is in fact a *thought object* beyond physics, and under the command of metaphysics. It is truth substance accessible and intelligible to us, and to which, (creatively), we add properties. It is their intelligibility, their truth 'compossibility', albeit an abstraction, that we adorn, as we will, with ears and tails (in representation of actual animals in the sensory world, that are themselves intelligible as sensible objects anyway).

In support of this we have the proverbial sense object of an onion, for example. We may well wonder, when we strip fruits of their attributes, (skin and flesh, as with apples and peaches), and we arrive at what we can 'read' as the thing's substance, its core or its stone, why the same is not so with the onion, for, as one philosopher observes, stripping it of its leaves, there is nothing left that *can* compose any substance.

The onion is our redemption, for it demonstrates how the substance of something, which normally we think to reach by the stripping of its attributes, cannot, in this case, physically be demonstrated. Its essence is not physical. It follows that the fault is our own *expectation* for the onion to have some physical and observable substance, instead of, what is more likely, that it is the *abstract intelligibility of the object that truly is its substance.*

The onion is an intelligible and sensible indicator of its own *essence*, self-evidential of it's 'being'. It has no dependence or reliance on some substance by physics, like having a core or stone that can offer opportunity to be *misconstrued* as truth substance or essence by the materialist. When he strips it of its skin and leaves, nothing remains to which these properties and attributes can be 'glued'.

Having observed this is so, material philosophy suggests that essence or substance has credibility in such an object *only by means of* its composition of properties and attributes. The truth being of the onion is sacrificed altogether by stubborn clinging to truth and reality as derived from physics, while clearly it is not possible that physics alone are sufficient to unchanging and unending true being when they are themselves a closed system directed to entropy. This is a 'sleight of mind' to avoid difficulty posed by the fact that there is required some *truth* being *object* to which properties can be said to apply.

What is more, it is not the physical onion but an object of *abstraction* we contemplate, whether or not we actually look at or think of a physical onion. This supports the idea that the true reality of any given *sensible* thing lies more probably in *mental life*, and what is *intelligible* about it, (its true substance), rather than in what may be, and more often is not, *observable*, or what physically may suggest itself as 'substance'.

An immediate bonus drops in our lap from such an approach, for, as we suppose to this point, if a thing is true and real, it is so *always*, and not just in any physical phase of existence in life, a period only of physics, with which it presents. Of course, if the substance of the true and real *is* its intelligibility, this supports, self evidently, that this, being independent of physics, *cannot* in truth degenerate, grow old, deteriorate, decay, or change in any way, for it is not commanded by any of the demons of physics, and especially time. This in no way requires us to rely solely on the 'prototype' of the 'intelligible world' of Plato, where all things of phenomena are mere 'appearances or representations'. Sensible things are *inclusive* to the whole of truth, and not altogether separable in this way.

Without a physical thing being present, it is impossible to observe it, and it would not exist at all unless it was intelligible, and therefore meaningful. However, *because* of its intelligibility, (its unending true meaning), it can certainly be contemplated by thought, at any time, even when it cannot be observed, though it could never, anyway, ever be observable *without* being essentially intelligible. Even memory and dreams can only present us with intelligible 'things' rather than physical ones. Just as well perhaps we do not wake to find the 'props' of our dream surrounding the bed.

Having come this far, it is both reasonable and consistent, to determine that we have sufficient justification to infer that, truly, there is much more about all 'things' than actually the eye alone encounters. It is not what is observable of something that makes it credible, and real, but the truth underwriting it. After all, the eye dwells in the world of sensory things, a world crammed with sensible objects, whether fruits, animals, buildings, or people. As we find in our case of the onion, all things *must* degenerate, due to their spatiotemporal confinement. However, and importantly, it is not physical presence, which is sufficient to present anything as true and *real* 'thing', but its meaning, which is only ascertainable by its *substantive significance*, and this is not sensory at all, but intelligible.

This is not an isolated view, and philosophy presents us with much support to deflect any criticism of excessive subjectivity, or unbridled imagination, the most recent being the work of Gabriel Marcel, in his *Etre et Avoir* of 1935, where he separates life and existence, from *being*, the one sensory, the other non sensory. But in addition to this, we have substance and essence issues from Aristotle, appearance and reality from Plato, the 'absolute idea' of Hegel, touching on the incompleteness of any one thing-in-itself, and similar issues raised by Kant. Of course there is also the duality of the human individual, as contributed by

Descartes, which supports appreciation of there being *two ways of viability* in any *one* particular 'thing'.

Without seeming to realise it, Berkeley stands at the threshold of what I suggest to be the true case, that all individual things have justified presence in two dimensions, (as object of *thing* and as object to *thought*), when he seems to slam the door shut on this. Without any adequate explanation of what he means, anyway, by the term 'mental', according to Russell, he 'relies' on the notion that 'everything must be *either* material *or* mental, and that nothing is both'. Of course what I suggest is quite contrary to this, for I am persuaded that all things *are* both.

Further to this, in referring to 'mental' things, I take him to mean objects of thought which are unavoidably intelligible, and my argument thus far implies that nothing can be understood anyway, or be meaningful, however richly we may perceive physical properties suggesting it is a 'sensible' thing, *unless* it is intelligible. I hope to demonstrate exactly this in what follows.

I may encounter a sheet of paper covered in interlocking scribbles, such as a child may perform. When I observe this sheet, at first I may take it to be something written or drawn on the paper. In other words, my first impression raises an expectation in me of something intelligible, but intelligible in the restricted context sense of my expectation of writing or drawing.

With closer scrutiny, I come to see that as writing or drawing it is 'unintelligible', (so that both my impression and my expectation are wrong), but as 'something' is on the paper, my argument suggests, that as it presents as *something* physically true and real, if this is truly so, it must present not only in physical form as *something*, but if real and true, must be also something intelligible in the sense of true. On conjoinment with its intelligibility as 'something', it becomes clear it is 'scribble', and even *scribble is something intelligible to me.* Logos again articulates. Anything that can *be* must be *something* seems to echo Parmenides.

The scribble on this page presents as a physical phenomenon, but, regardless of any impressions or expectations I may have of it presenting in *whatever* sensible form to me, (as writing or drawing for example), if truly it *does* present itself, then must it be intelligible, or it can be nothing. In addition to this, the ink used may fade, or the paper may be burned, so that in sensible 'form' it can 'exist' no longer, and this would make it unreal as anything that *ever* presented, except for the fact that as it *is* intelligible, (significant, true and real, and a fragment to the sum total all things that can ever be), it cannot ever cease to be. (Rather like a fact), it is therefore always accessible as an object to thought. Once presenting as intelligible and real, it cannot change or cease to *be* something, (though its physical counterpart may cease to *exist*). I can contemplate it even when it does *not* exist.

Here I wish to demolish the objection of language philosophers to what I have summoned above, in terms of 'scribble', 'writing', or 'drawing'. The argument I make is not based on language use, for whether we were familiar with these words or not, such words as *writing* or *scribble* are a codified expression *after* an encounter with phenomena and noumena. Except for my having to resort to language here to *describe* the interface of these, there is no dependence on language other than describing events. The same understandings are accessible without the use of language. A term used in Art education for this is *haptic*; this describes the facility of grasping something without semiotics or language codes. It implies also an immediacy that these do not always demonstrate.

This principle is amply demonstrated in non-figurative or 'abstract' artwork, where the artist uses visual and tactile *language* to pioneer form, texture, colour, etc., which itself, is the object we encounter in the physical world, and where it makes no reference, even by association, with sensible things of which already there are earthly instances.

While I am experiencing *life*, and existing, one class of 'things' intelligible, as individual *personhood* to me, is that of people about me. Another may be that of some building. Such things may *cease to exist* during my lifetime, as physical things, but as they are required as fragments to all that can be true and real, and as they are always to be intelligible, (and in spite of ceasing to *exist*), they cannot therefore *cease to be.*

Parmenides is the first champion of this resonant notion. They will always be accessible to thought, even when I, suffering from dementia or some defect, cannot think of them. Their being, as true and intelligible things, is wholly independent of my mind, or whether I can, or do, focus on them, and whether or not I can *know* of them *by* memory or reflection of any kind. Primarily, it is because *always* they are there, that any focus by me is made possible. They have essential being. This is the principle employed by St Anselm, when he prompts us with what follows.

He starts with the question of what object of thought we can have which can be the *greatest* of all thoughts. This is obliged to be an object of abstraction. We may at first choose many things, but whatever that can be, we can be sure that it can only be something intelligible, for otherwise we could not think it. He follows this prompt with others, along the lines that if what we choose was not possible for some reason to ensnare, what then could be even greater than that, until we arrive at the notion he himself anticipates in his questioning; God. Nothing, he asserts, can be greater than that, as object to thought.

What is interesting of course, is that for such an object to thought to be viable, it must be intelligible, and for the Christian, like St Anselm, there is more, for not only can the intelligible object be accessed by the act of thinking, its counterpart, as sensible object, and in a world of sensory things, is also, historically, accessible; the human personification and sensible object of particular personhood, as counterpart, to the intelligible but amorphous 'thing' of God; the Christ figure. We are presented with 'two sides of one coin, again, and no other world faith offers this.

A 'sure and certain' comfort arises from such a way of thought, as Thomas More suggests, in that in the intelligibility of things, whether sensible, or thought, lays the assurance of a divine extension of *being* to all things. This has nothing whatever to do with their material and physical composition, but with their *intelligible authenticity*, as truth and reality. Whether they exist now, (that is in time or space), has no affect on this *unchanging* state, and this is convergent with the work of Gabriel Marcel. Centuries of machination by great thinkers from Parmenides, through Avicenna, (with his emphatic reliance on thought as a primary energiser of *everything*), and the perennial notion of the 'logos', or the principle of intelligibility, are all-supportive of this one encouraging theme.

What I wish to add to the contributions of these renowned thinkers, however it may be thought to border on mysticism, is the overtly spiritual contribution, convergent with such thinking as that above, by Christ, when personally present. For my own part, I detect something surprisingly close, in spite of its spiritual intent, to matters that concern physics and metaphysics, rather than a marginal theology alone. There is striking convergence with the theme I present here in His little known sayings, as promulgated in my appendix on the Gospel of St Thomas. It may more be associated with the rational, (however lyrically expressed), than the 'fideist' tradition. This is my own rebellious contribution, in the face of ever-resurgent materialism.

Scrutiny of this appendix reveals a decisive synchronicity between the gospel's distinction between *motion and rest* and any consideration of *physics and metaphysics*. Things we may describe as in *motion and constant flux*, and things *at rest* and ultimate resolution that is unchanging, fixed and rigid, as is truth. This synchronicity, along with what is implied by *contemplation*, or meditation, is to be the ultimate closure of my philosophy of feeling theme.

Chapter 8 – Motion and Rest

Man's living and existing requires social criteria while it is his being requires values. The one is commanded by motion, the other by rest. Both engage us daily, one ever shifting, the other ever fixed.

Motion is the dynamic of physics as they resolve their route to entropy, and as far as we understand, it originates in the creation of the universe at the point of singularity we evocatively call the 'big bang'. It is by motion that stars, planets, plants and animals, not to mention man, with his extraordinary intelligence, are charged with life and energy, within parameters of time and space, things *also* derivative of that same singularity and creative instant. Until that instant there is undisturbed and omnipresent *rest*, as always there is until *motion*, the energiser and impulse power of physics, disturbs it. Borrowing from Schopenhauer, we may even say that creation, (physics), disturbs the 'blessed calm' of non-existence, (metaphysics).

This is not so bleak as at first it may strike us, for in the manner of our use here, 'existence' is a thing of physics, but it is *being* that is the vitalism of metaphysics, as we have seen by abstract entities we encounter daily, as accessed by thought. We therefore have a way of *knowing* that however 'coming to be, or going', to or from existence and life bodies can be said to be, their *essence* as things of truth and reality cannot change or end. Universals, such as philosophers engage, and artists attempt to image, as with whiteness and forms of beauty; mathematics and number, and geometric forms, with no place in physics otherwise, etc. are further examples of unchanging *truth*, that are ubiquitous to mental life.

Beyond any second point of singularity there may be, where motion may dissipate on any collapse of the universe, the *same* rest awaits from which it emerged anyway. 'T'was ever thus!' repeats. This is the eternal region beyond physics, as we may infer, to either side of motion and physics, and abiding throughout them also, for all things that have *being*, including physics and motion themselves, are within the gift of metaphysics. Nothing can *be* of *truth and reality* without either motion or rest, or both, to support it. With motion. there is physics, with rest there is metaphysics. Motion and physics are of descending hierarchy from metaphysic accreditation (and origin) of the *being of all true or significant things*.

In any single identifiable object, even of the sensible and sensory variety, what may be considered the *moveables* of it must be distinguished from the *being of truth* that constitutes its place in reality. The motion of physics in things cannot alone provide expectation or assurance of extensive durability. For this purpose, I make use of a celebrated example from philosophy of the restoration of the sailing ship Cutty Sark that occupies an undoubted place in reality. To do this it is first necessary to consider the ship's nature as a sensible object, and its place in truth.

As we see later this primary 'place' is not geophysical or a 'place' and location in the normal way the word is used, in terms of physics. Though it may not have been his intention, even the giant of philosophy, Plato, allows a substitute tactile 'place' of *imagery* to be adopted by his construct of the 'intelligible world'. In this way we are obliged to imagine an observable 'place', (in the normal meaning of this), for something that is, rather more accurately, a very real and necessary *zone of being*, however abstracted altogether from physical constructs of any kind; one of metaphysics. What may be more readily cognisant of this is a sort of 'baseboard' or elemental support to all that is real, not some seemingly likely construct of 'invention' as we may envisage an island or territory.

Truth has no size, no shape, no weight, nor any property of physics. Yet even without any physics, it is something imperative *in the world of physics*, and this shows it to be *necessary*. We must recognise it therefore as a necessary and real thing even though it is an abstraction. It follows that if there is to be any true and real thing in the world, its truth gives it abstract foundation making it possible for it to *exist* at all. Clearly truth is greater and primary to anything of physics, and, however abstract, and unobservable, is intelligible to 'mind'.

This implies that truth *and* intelligibility are under direct command of the metaphysical principle. Both are abstractions, and neither are of subjective origination. In addition by such cognition between intelligible abstractions, and our apprehension *of* them, it is clear that *mind* of some extensive order, (Logos), permeates everything to which our individual mind is merely a *part*. As some philosophy indicates, a sensible object of physics does not disappear when any individual human mind can no longer contemplate it.

Furthermore, truth is always what it is, is unchangeable, and is in an imponderable and ethereal state of *rest*. This abstract location, impenetrable and inaccessible to physics or its derivatives, as a state of rest, cannot be known and understood as we know and understand physical things. Yet however we try or fail to describe it, it is intelligible to us as a *brute fact*, regardless of its presenting only as an abstraction. Its opacity to complete understanding is insufficient to disenfranchise it.

Always what we contemplate as an object of thought must be unambiguously clear and distinct. Though there may well be in the world an instance of physics with which a given object of abstraction may be associated, the former necessarily presents a 'thing' of physics that is not the same thing as the object of abstraction. The one may be erased from physics, while the other abides always, with its identity wholly intact.

In the restoration of the vessel Cutty Sark, all physical components of the ship are likely to be, ultimately, replaced, and therefore not likely to be the original components of the physical Cutty Sark. The ship is subject to change as it is subject to the laws of physics. The ship at P1, and T1, (position and time of first place), cannot be the identical ship of P2 and T2, (second location). How can we claim the ship of first event is identical to the ship of the second? How are we to say that the ship at all particular instants of time, and in all places of space, is the one ship that is contemplated? Precisely the same benchmark must be applied to human identity and personhood.

The importance of our reply to this cannot be overstated. Unless the Cutty Sark is of truth standing, (the clear metaphysical 'brute fact'), it could never adopt the physical properties necessary to *be* an object of sense and *exist* in the physical world at all. Without 'true being' it has no physical existence as a 'thing'. Truth is a pre-requisite of all sensible objects. As it has clearly presented as such, it is both an intelligible object of truth which is unalterable, (and this can be contemplated by mind), and an intelligible sensible object of the world, that can change, (and *this* too can be contemplated by mind, as well as experienced by the senses).

At all particular instants of time, (something of physics), and in all particular places of space, (again something of physics), it is not different ship-identities that are encountered, but one particular identity of ship, for always it carries the authenticity and credentials of *abstract* contemplative provenance that sustains the *being* of an unchanging truth. The fact that physical timbers or parts of it differ from the original timbers and parts is a physical *bye product* of its presentation under the command of physics. This has no affect whatsoever on the *truth object* that supports it, and is *always* accessible by contemplation. The phenomenal ship is a *moveable*, the noumenal ship is not.

Precisely the same principle applies when we compare the completely different situation of what we regard as 'ethics' and what we regard as 'values'. If dissatisfied by gender distinction which nature bestows, regarding it as responsible for certain inconveniences, we may think to remove the inconveniences by removing the distinction. In so doing we may invent some androgynous alternative of an ethical culture of 'unisex'. We prefer to contemplate a fiction rather than a fact, rather than aspiring to the virtue of cherishing a distinction nature can alone authorise.

Perceived standards of correctness, repeatedly changing and reappraised, are 'moveables' associated with *behaviourism* of practical application. As cultures themselves change, so also do these 'ethics'. They concern pragmatics and utility, matters concerned with physical living and experience, so that what is always contemplated is some contingent of physical circumstance or a condition that may be thought open to improvement. As we see amply demonstrated, the primary concern always of ethics is living and experience, and often we will self applaud this as a virtue that often it clearly is not.

Of course however steps may be taken in this way even with the best of intention, satisfying outcome cannot be guaranteed, and in fact is often counterproductive. By assent and adoption in relation to an ethic of racial purity, as employed by the Third German Reich, and observed by its executive and judicial authority, attempts were made of a mandatory 'goodness' that was hopelessly in error. After the world conflict accompanying it, this inhuman and embarrassing outcome was unavoidably castigated. The clear reason for such reversal of what is intended is the impoverished quality of judgement from which such agreed measures derive. *Ethics in general emerge from human judgement* and are fallible.

This may well lead us to ask if human judgement is so unreliable, what other resource may we look to in the hope of improving our decision-making. To those who have not desensitised themselves from it, there is unarguable alternative resource that should be tapped into at times of decision-making.

However we describe this facility, such as instinct, intuition, conscience, etc., it is rooted in our capacity for spontaneous recognition of all sensory things lying between 'poles'. We all demonstrate our capacity of instant recognition when we are repelled *by reflex* so that we 'feel' disgust. Equally do we recognise instantly what brings great joy. Such judgement does not have to depend on levels of *experience in life.*

The poles may best be understood as spanning the gap between what is positive and welcoming to us, and what is negation of this or repellent to us. A beautiful aroma may lead us on, while the sight of blood may drive us away. To all of us there is an innate desire for goodness and wholesomeness, beauty, wisdom, dignity and such like.

At the same time we are driven to escape wickedness, ugliness, ignorance, and self-pride. We are so well prepared to encounter such things that even on our first encounter what we feel about things has immediacy, and this in turn suggests *foreknowledge,* that we should so instantly recognise one or another. Some philosophy indicates this as evidence of 'a priori' knowledge.

We show by our repulsion or our attraction to things, from infant and inexperienced times, to old age, that we cherish some things and despise others, and *without* prior training. We have cherishment, affection, and love for some, revulsion and disgust for others. Unless severely disordered, we are not ultimately content to be drawn to something we despise. When this 'feeling' we have in response to something is utilised as a resource for judgement and decision-making, we have by it a natural inclination to virtue, and *values in relation to virtue* inform decisions and judgements as a matter of course. We have a conclusion grounded in *morality,* and no ethic carries this power. We have drawn together our reasoning and our emotion, and *this,* always satisfying, leads in turn to contentment and self-assurance.

In our daily lives we perform many 'acts of thought', and these always focus on a particular 'object of contemplation'. If many others distract certain acts of thought, requiring *differing* objects of contemplation that crowd in on us at once, we cannot resolve ourselves on any one in particular. We cannot help but be indecisive and unresolved. We cannot in these circumstances be at peace with ourselves. Such a peace is best achieved when we discipline our acts of thought to engage by intellective *and* emotional input coalescing into a *single* order.

In the pursuit of what we may describe as happiness or contentment, in the lives of human individuals, the greatest measure of this is found by far in those whose chief object of contemplation is neither happiness nor contentment. We may see the truth of this in any scrutiny of a variety of individuals, such as saints, accountants, sculptors, or generals. Those who can be said to be most successful at acquiring contentment or happiness are usually those whose *chief* object of contemplation is something *other* than these things altogether, and a harmony of *self with otherness.*

Such fortunates may be said to possess a subliminal awareness of the metaphysic principle, (operating like 'apperception'), making sensible things of physics incomplete to them, as being insufficient alone as a reliable source of meaning, and that more than things themselves is required. Their primary focus is not on *things* at all, but what things signify, infer, or imply, in terms of *meaning.* As there are no built in labels to 'things', often this will call for careful rumination. Indeed, they cherish meaning beyond 'things' leading to evaluation. Those with sufficient insight presuppose significance to *belong* under the metaphysic principle, not to the physics. This favours their execution of their values with a view to clinging to lasting virtue.

This procedure may often be most inconvenient if we look only to comfort and pleasure of a sensory nature in the world of living and experiencing. The reason for this lies with what is absent from our contemplation; the pursuit of virtue by our values, which nourish, and are required by, our very real and true being, will often ignore convenience. We are touching on this when we claim our spirit is low. Something of virtue is missing and we feel deprived.

The chief object of contemplation for the saint is *not* happiness or contentment, but God. If it were otherwise he would forego torture. That of the accountant is the integrity of his accounting, by which he hopes to avoid gaol. For the sculptor, it is his creative impulse to express an idea, escaping from a silence intolerable to him, and for the general it is the satisfaction of achieving some strategic or tactical resolution of a military task in serving an ideal. Indeed, it may be said that those who make their chief object of contemplation happiness or contentment are the most likely to review their lives and experience as traumatic, disenchanting, and in some cases, so dismal an experience, as to warrant suicide.

In the same way, if our objects of contemplation are centred on our physical existence, (*motion*), we are the more likely, as I declared at the beginning of this book, to face 'restlessness built into everything short of death'. It is clear that there is more satisfaction to be drawn in our lives from some object of contemplation of a more permanent and spiritual nature than anything of a passing physical variety; something more in relation to a position of *rest*.

This does not necessarily mean that we must devote ourselves entirely to religious zeal, as may be supposed, but we do require something of spiritual outlook, where values toward virtue play an enriching part. Religions inevitably tend to mechanise this aspiration by promoting fixed methods and procedures. Spiritual awareness however *is required*, as we may intuit from *life and experience* by creative pursuits of imagination, invention, or problem solving, and as we encounter astronomy, mathematics, science, philosophy, or the composition of music. Without the spiritual element of our *being* in its devotion to virtue playing some part in our *life and experience*, we cannot be complete in person.

If a man's chief object of contemplation is 'ethics' and their criteria suggest in error what is good, he is often likely to be operating amorally and only in the arena of living and existing, and therefore *motion*. If he follows such direction without feeling it appeals within him to his own interests, he may also lead an inauthentic life. His opposite number may well in contrast constantly ruminate on 'virtue' suggesting what is *unchangeably* good, and he is exercising spirit of *being*, engaging with ever-fixed things of *rest*, not as criteria, but as absolutes. He also leads his life with a degree of self-authenticity. Not much assiduity is required to see which of the two individuals is the more likely to be content.

In my opening to this work I stressed the importance of self worth tempered by humility and love, and attributed the sense of fellowship which arises from this as typified in the cultural renaissance in which mid twentieth century Liverpool art culture played a conspicuous part. This rebellion as I referred to it, *dismantled* ethical custom, which had little appeal to them, yet respected the private dignity accessible to us all as quantified individual worth. By so doing it attributed 'value' to human 'being' *during* living and experiencing, *beyond* merely the practical lives we lead, and bearing relation to the *virtues*, (as true *values* do), and our regard for each other.

Such an attitude epitomized the 'bohemian life' there, though carrying an appearance of 'carelessness' to the socially conformist, and ethical thinker. In fact it signified the opposite, a spiritual awareness of something greater than mere custom and agreed so-called 'norms'. Popular music of the time picked up only on ready-made themes to emphasise rejection of these norms, but lacked the depth of the artists' cause.

Such aspirational things as the art life of Liverpool espoused at the time are derived of awareness of true benevolence and good, a worthiness in ourselves *and* our fellows, (far more profound than the political wit and collective assumption of democracy, or the cursory reading made by reinvention of pop music). As I have asserted already, such elemental change cannot arise simply from assertion, some 'notice board' type code of ethics. Rebels opposing social repression did more than this. They destroyed ethical criteria reverenced before. Ethics, as I have suggested already, are man made things, and can be as capricious as the variety of collective authority which exercises sufficient power to enforce them, from the society of Rome, to that of the Third German Reich.

Values that emerge from ethics are not 'values' per se, but *accepted* standards of correctness that have no guarantee of truth to them, and, as history demonstrates, the foolish criteria by which false or counterfeit 'values' are established, are often a source of embarrassment to many, and often hurriedly revised. This oft repeated procedure can be nourished by the misplaced notion that in 'change' there is always improvement, when often the reverse is so. Ethics today suggest *woman* has the 'right' to violate the child in her womb. Values *always* suggest, whatever the century, that the injustice of such an act is so *self-evident*, that any such claimed right, is pure fiction. The ethic is designed to meet a *convenience* of whatever variety.

The reason for such confused thinking, (not unlike losing ones compass in the desert), stems from the widespread ignorance of what, *actually*, values truly are, and from which they derive, and for this reason I feel it appropriate that I should restate their true import, as defined in my first book of the philosophy of feeling series.

As I declared then, values are things which concern how we *feel* towards whatever we contemplate, (even if that is with regard to each other), and I say that 'either we cherish what we contemplate, and therefore value it highly, or, because what we contemplate *is* valued highly, (by others, or society in general), we *then* cherish it'. For whatever reason, if something repels and disgusts us it is unlikely to be a thing we can cherish, even when maligned for not doing so. If it *is* that we cherish a thing, we value something *for its own sake,* but if the second reason above, (because it *is* what is cherished), then truly what we value is 'human opinion'.

The woman's 'right' we describe above, attending human opinion, is far removed from love and virtue, and is grounded in the self-interest of the commanding agent alone. When we are led by what we cherish, this leads us to values that are authentic, meaningful and very real in our lives, and may easily be associated with unbounded love, while often only confused thinking leads to ethics, which may be upheld or discarded, and are unstable.

Ethics and morality are distinguishable as entirely different things, as already I have attempted to highlight. While ethics concern culture, custom, collective outlook, adoptive attitude, and such like, morality only selectively informs these things, and moral purpose may not be of primary importance to a given collective. The aspiration to serve virtue alone, (and not some *other* standard of correctness that others may suggest to us), is morality's primary objective, while not necessarily the objective of ethics. Ethics often concern pragmatic aspects of living and experiencing, (motion), while morality serves virtue and peace, (rest). One is of material concern, the other abstract.

Both in private or public practice, moral judgement, as to what is desirable with deferment to virtue, or what is good, (and with regard for what is contrary to virtue, and therefore bad), is the sole way of life for private and public self worth to resist collapse into barbarism. The power of *discrimination* in this is essential. Ethics, which do not necessarily take their lead from a regard for morality, and what virtue requires of us, (today's ethics even condemn discrimination itself), cannot carry the credentials and authenticity, intrinsic to clinging to virtue, which *alone* is the one worthy contemplative object of morality.

Those of us driven by soulful craving for ultimate benevolence and good in all things are those of whom it may be said have predilection to cling to virtue, even without instruction. If they must resist ethical codes to do so, then they will. Values such as *they* cherish, the *self-evident virtues,* are the base line and grounding, and chief object of contemplation to them, in the way they conduct their lives. No substitute standards of correctness that may interrupt or disturb this *internal* harmony are readily tolerated.

Paradigms of this are available to us in history where 'heroes' are known as such only by their sometime courageous stance against overwhelming odds. They have no interest in, and will oppose, any contravention of virtue, even on just or intrusive law. This brings us to reconsider exactly what these values are, as outlined at the onset of this chapter, and in what way they may be considered 'self-evident'.

We are at liberty to say that *true* values, (as against standards of correctness adopted through ethics), may be regarded as naturally imperative to the well being of the spirit of man, in part by the evidence of history and tradition. Even in the ancient classical world of Greece and Rome, we have reliance upon the virtues of *wisdom, fortitude,* (or courage), *faith,* (investing love and loyalty), *temperance,* (or moderation), and, of course, *justice.* There is well-defined value of these things both in the individual and in any collective state, and we have already seen how they inform judgement.

Christianity later elected *hope, charity,* and *love,* to the same philosophic attitude. 'Ethics man' may well object here that we inherit no obligation to follow the ways of our forbears, but we are just as free to ask is this because he cannot love those forebears, or even show them charity. It is after all *our* love of *them,* and *their* love of *us,* their children, which surely is the very employment of values, derived of virtues, that it seems are being so readily dismissed.

However badly at times in history our forbears may have borne themselves, confusedly, as to the virtues, and values that serve them, privately they could have no doubt that indeed they existed and were significant to their lives. This is clear both through historical revision made, and by what defines the greatest of arts. On the private epistemic route of course, we have dealt with repulsion and attraction, and intuitive knowledge. Unjust and uncaring laws known to be so at the time, however recommended by ethics, or derivative of them, cannot be attributed to virtue.

In responding to how it may be seen that virtue promotes innate direction within us, and is thereby self evident, it is also fair to say that it is only through clinging to virtue, benevolence and the good, with submission and sincerity, that we feel a wholeness of personhood. If sensitised sufficiently by the apperception I have alluded to already, we find ourselves empowered within to smile, give encouraging word, or offer kindnesses to another. This clearly arises from clinging to a virtue arising from our value of what we cherish in our fellows, and our submission to love. Giver and receiver, granting peace to both, engage goodness and virtue.

Generally, observance of values required to attain a harmony of nature, is itself self-fulfilling, providing even in a turbulent life of experience, enlightened and often uninterrupted levels of rest, creating a peace and harmony of spirit, both emotive and intellective. Those of us who shine in such a way in effect enrich their lives and the lives of others by inviting the metaphysic principle into the physical world. Rest and assurance in heart and mind ejects fears and anxieties.

Though this may be attacked for its blatant 'consequentialism' or utility, it can only be said that if it is *that*, it is of an entirely *spiritual* sort. It is abstract application of thought to abstract entities, under the metaphysic principle. There is no guarantee of physical comfort and ease to accompany it. The greatest aid to us in achieving such a peace is that of abject honesty, both towards our fellows and ourselves, a practice more familiar to generations less spiritually impoverished, while often more physically underprivileged.

An ethical principle may well be adopted to kill the young or the old, (e.g. abortion and euthanasia), in devotion to some misplaced sentiment, for example, that this would be good for society as a whole. By the removal of homosexuality from criminal law, it is argued, homosexuals lead a more convenient life, without risk of public censure or question, *itself* criminalised instead. All of this, along with such a measure as outlawing corporal punishment of intemperate youth, addresses the liberty, ease and comfort of any individual to do as he pleases, or as he wills. It does nothing to address virtues such as temperance or love.

No legitimacy is granted to methods of persuading the transgressors of virtue otherwise by such excessively liberal an approach, so that only convenience and comfort is in effect the object contemplated. All of this is yet incompletely and undigested *ethical procedure,* applied in our time, and assuring, by its lack of moral input or purpose, an inevitable and impending threat of nightmare proportions as a legacy that we are in justice deserving.

Morality, or the leading of a virtuous life, quite a different thing, is *not* what is today generally contemplated. This distinction is necessary for astute determination of what may be preferred. Debate on such matters as tribal origin, race, or homosexuality, is itself, however, now to be regarded as *prejudice*, ill-conceived discourtesy, and even best proscribed by law. A *tyrannical ideology hostile to thinking men*, but it seems, we are expected to perceive it as a glowing democratic achievement.

However well intended, or by some perverse line of reasoning, or misplaced sentiment, one may attempt to justify such things as those above, clearly such ethical lines of extreme liberalism are unconcerned with any principle of morality. Their chief object of contemplation has more natural kinship with pragmatics and convenience. The chief object contemplated by such ethical measures and fortified by law, is what is *perceived* as measures to make life circumstances more convenient for men, however virtuous or otherwise. True values, of any meaning and truth, are the concern of *morality*, and are unaffected by the vagaries so engaging to ethics, which more concerns itself with what is 'politick', and *desired.*

Reliably then, we may conclude that ethics are based upon human agreement, negotiation, or assent, in *perceiving* what is received as 'good', (or, more precisely, *desirable*), and, generally, good in terms of *convenient*. Values, in contrast, associated with morality, are direct mediators of virtue, or good itself, which is clearly not the same thing. Ethics rely upon opinions and perceptions, while values, if they are to be meaningful, originate only from virtue, good itself.

Values require no justification or appraisal, as they are both intuitive, timelessly universal, and prior to *all* meaningful thought or action. Negotiation on them is irrelevant, though vigorous training of the young to acknowledge what they feel already to be goodness is prudent, so to help them avoid error. This too would today seem abandoned by either instruction or example.

What is perhaps more important to my argument is that ethics have natural affinity with the levels of convenient collective well being, as pragmatics demand. Lascivity is unbounded; while true values have natural affinity with what is best described as an authentic and privately acquired sense of inner peace and rest. The ergodynamism of this promotes a 'custom made' and individual centred stability and sense of well being, and virtue being a universal property accessible to all, if all were to embrace it, there would be no need for any 'notice board' of ethics.

In addition to this, while ethics, devoted to the human condition in life, are as capricious as the societies adopting them, they are subject, (as are all things concerning life and existence in a physical world), to revision and change, while this is *not* so in the case of morality, which directly interfaces with unchanging virtue, and the good. Virtue, to which values are directly 'hinged', is something *intelligible*, (*mediation* between ourselves and our surroundings), and not sensory, and has no relation to 'conveniences' in life, or collective expedient living.

As such it is rigid and exact, and an unchanging truth. Courage or temperance, (such values as are directly associated with good and virtue), are no different today than they were in 3000BC, while ethics of then and now bear little comparison. It would be anathema today to compass human opponents fight to the death for public amusement, though, it seems, this now is regarded as normality in the undisciplined streets of our towns.

Ethics and morality are clearly two very *different* things, and where any distinction is ignored, psychological, emotional, and intellective disarray threatens the order that is to be expected of any civilised collective. We experience this today with confusion everywhere with its resultant damage, as may be expected. Particularly is this evident in the young, who generally display all the symptoms of private and social insecurity, and the neurosis or anxiety that is the natural outcome of irresponsible and confused leadership, without any reliable guidance, or feeling of certainty to offer.

Ignorance, (often the target of Charles Dickens' work), is today even more released from its cage, and wholly unobstructed, lurks in the streets. The virtues, which *could* provide stability, are distinctly out of favour, 'uncool', (in proverbial 'zip' language), and embarrassing to mention for the present. 'Let archbishops who cannot tow the line with what is *desired*, hold their tongue' is the implied wisdom. Comparing this sentiment with other places and times where it is familiar should cause concern even to the prudent secularist.

Rather than dwelling on this tragic scenario however, I wish to proceed to connect morality, the pursuit of values required by virtue, and the position of ultimate rest, the things beyond physics constituting ultimate reality. To do this adequately, it is necessary to refer again to the dual experience offered to us while living and experiencing, and encountering 'things', (of the sensory world), while being engaged *simultaneously* by means of thought, with 'things' that are intelligible, which may, or may not, present as sensible and physical *also*. The first, living and experiencing, concerns *life*, for a *given* time, while the second, concerns *being*, which obtains in perpetuity.

Chapter 9 – The Forced Issue of Metaphysics

No other but we ourselves authenticate or create where we come to rest.
Observed things are events of the world. Events of mind are unobservable.

Operating a literary licence, when it is advised 'forget the future, and look to the past with absolute confidence', clearly reliance is being placed on what is *known* to be established *truth*. In this case it is 'things', (whether sensible objects, events, or persons), of which there are known instance in the past. Besides their mode of physics, as *phenomena*, they are *also* known 'things' as *truth objects*, (abstractions).

We have both presences as things of phenomena, that end, and presences of objects of truth, beyond physics of time and place, that cannot. We easily recognise in things past, *passing things,* as phenomena, but also *everlasting things* as truth objects. Clearly the truth object is greater than the object of phenomena by its perpetuity alone, and this distinguishes the greater significance of being a truth object over that of physical existing. There is *perpetuity in the abstraction* but *transience in the sensible,* even where what is perceived and what is conceived is the same object of contemplation.

We may have expectation of things 'out there', perceivable or conceivable, physical or metaphysical, that may *become known* as true, though they cannot *be* known so until we reach a future time. *What* we know, and *when* we know it, are evolutionary states of consciousness through passage of time, and these are things of physics. Things of *truth being* are *not* objects (or entities) of physics, but *are* entities of abstraction within metaphysics. We are very prepared to compass this gap, to treat them as *apprehendable,* (tomorrow a child can be born, or the universe may end), even though we have no idea in whatever manner, or at whatever 'now' moment, whether, or *even if,* they may materialise as instances in physics.

Though we anticipate that *things of true being* may be *apprehendable,* and 'now', they do not *require* that they are comprehensively *knowable* 'now'. Clearly the *being* of a truth and the *knowing* of it are each distinctive from the other. Truth being can exist without knowledge of it, but knowledge of it can never exist without truth being prior to it. In the same way are we empowered to *apprehend* 'reality' in the order of *truth being* of entities under the metaphysical principle, without having to *know* them intimately as we may know physical 'things'. Awareness of metaphysics is more a matter of sensitivity and inner apprehension, to greater or lesser degree, than a matter of cognition, experience or knowledge, as certainly applies to physics.

It follows that if one forgets an episode or instant of experience, or an object of thought, this does not make it either untrue or unreal. Forgetting it is simply not *knowing* it, and we have seen already that something does not require to be known in order to be true. Memory, likewise, has no power to qualify a thing as true, and is no more instrumental than knowledge or forgetting. Independently of these, a thing may be true and real, and therefore always a 'brute fact'. It is independent of, though accessible to, mental life.

Memory or knowledge as we see has no affect on what *cannot* become untrue, what does *not* change, and what pertains *always*. A thing's being is its sole required qualification. To be recognised, (another form of *knowing*), any 'truth object', whether abstract or material, must be sufficient to any test of scrutiny, whether this is based on acquaintance, description, or reasoned judgement. Its' *being* is an abstraction, not something of the world of physics, so that verification based on *them* is not a prerequisite. Our knowledge, (to which memory is a party), mindset, and whether we are introspective or retrospective, simply does not come into the matter.

I would remind the reader here of our encounter with the distinction earlier between retrospection, (memory or recollecting), and introspection, (ruminating on some object of immediate contemplation). While the first concerns what always lies *behind*, and may concern object of *thing* in past time, in spacetime, (though we certainly re-encounter it *now*), introspection or self-examination can be timeless, explorative, and at liberty to ignore time. This fluidity of mental life is not confined solely to speculation when, not infrequently, and as we saw earlier in the drawings of Leonardo, by rumination it is perfectly possible to apprehend predictive truths, though what may be objectified by them may be unknown territory at any given moment or in any given place.

There are two objections to this metaphysical approach with which it is necessary to deal before reliable conclusions may be drawn. One is that as metaphysics are supposed to deal with things *beyond* and out of reach of physics, they cannot be other than pure speculation. The other is rooted in a widely received understanding of *truth* as something that we should expect fully to *know*, while all metaphysics can do is present theories and hypotheses suggesting that *truth* is a *being of things* that is undemonstrable, both because it is an abstraction and unquantifiable entity, and because, contrary to what we expect, it cannot wholly be known by the same token. No complete list of truth objects is possible.

Taking the latter case first, the *received* understanding of the 'nature of truth' is well represented by Bertrand Russell, when he elects truth as a 'property of beliefs or statements'. This implies that the existence of truth is mind-dependent, (truths as properties of beliefs), for he claims also that if there were no beliefs there could be neither truth nor falsehood. Rather than a *property* of beliefs and statements, *truth* is wholly independent of these. Beliefs are simply not necessary. Where they do recognise truth of course they are authentic for they are fragments of it. This is so whatever part mind or whatever part knowledge may have in such recognition. Therefore truth is not mind dependent.

Features of consciousness in relation to *knowledge*, (like beliefs), and truth *being* or *not*, as we have already seen, are completely different things. The abstract entity, (object of truth), that is a necessary fragment of the whole, is *not* mind-dependent, nor does it *require* to be known.

Russell goes on to declare that truth is 'some form of correspondence between belief and fact'. Correspondence, like coherence, is a conscious *mind relation* directed to 'things', while truth is independent altogether of any mind-related belief. A truth being is what it *is* independently of belief. In the last paragraph we see how he defines truth as some sort of 'property', and now we have this 'truth' relating to things and underwriting the authenticity of those things, so we have it as a *relation* as well.

Truth as a comprehensive totality of all that has authentic being is *more* than a property, or a relation, and is certainly something greater than individual minds or consciousness. Though we can have no whole knowledge of truth or the list of all true things, its being cannot be doubted. All that concerns Russell here is *knowledge and consciousness*, and not the *being of things as truth*, as metaphysics poses.

In his consideration of truth, he contemplates what is believed or known, and whatever this may be may also be true or false. This concerns accuracies or mistakes of conscious awareness. What we contemplate here differs in the way that whether or not we are conscious of anything, if truly something *is*, and may be said to have intelligible being, this is grounded in its presupposed impossibility *to be*, (of physical or abstract form), *unless* it is of truth.

The sole adequate or sufficient grasp of truth readily accessible to us, (even though this is not a comprehensive understanding of it, for this is veiled from us in our sensory surroundings of the world), is that for anything *to exist* or *to be*, its *substance* must lie with truth. Unlike Russell we are unconcerned with its having properties or relations, and coherence and convergence doesn't come into it at all. Truth is not some scale or measure against which things are to be compared, like some kind of plumbline. If a thing is to exist or to be, it *is* an object, (of sense data or abstraction), the substance of which *is* truth. *In brief, it is something.* Our consciousness of such a thing is secondary to this.

Truth is the supportive thread of uninterruptible and absolute being of metaphysical dimension, for unlike things of physics, it has no time or space, no beginning or ending, and is the authority underwriting all ontologies, physical or abstract. It is the pre-existent condition of origination to which all things owe their *being*. Without it there is no *substance* to anything, cognitive or not. Without it there is no *itness*, (form of identity), no justified belief, no facts, and no presences of anything. The occasion or instance of all things has foundation and significance only by its authorised *substance* underwritten by truth.

Undeniably, the being of things of abstraction must be engaged *throughout* physics while at the same time they are extensive *beyond* them, and primarily under the command only of the metaphysic principle. It is precisely in this way that virtue and goodness are self-revealing as necessary and self-evidential. By reasoning or revelation, always they are accessible to us as 'universals' simply by their uninterrupted and substantial *being*. Before considering universals it is necessary to deal with the first of our two objections to truth as metaphysic *being*.

Besides what we have said of truth as the authoriser of everything, this first objection implies that metaphysics cannot be other than pure speculation, as being *beyond* physics, theories and hypotheses cannot be adequately tested. This is very much an exaggerated pose, often stemming from lack of intuitive responsibility and the sensitivity to which I have referred. It is yet another case of applying verification procedures that are inappropriate beyond the field of physics. Also it ignores the necessity to recognise the actuality of abstractions, if life experience is to be meaningful.

First we need to recall how we can come to know of something, extending Russell's own criteria by just a fraction. He claims we can know of something by personal *acquaintance* with it, and by reliable *description* of it. As we may expect however, he does not lay equal stress on *reasoned judgement* as any sort of qualifier as to something we can *know*. It was, after all, by such means as these that mathematics delivered triangles to us, empowering us to reach the moon, and populate the New World and North Americas. Clearly persuasive judgements can be made by astute thought and reasoning, with any means of verification necessarily following behind. We are obliged to accept abstractions as entities of truth in our daily lives. The less astute our judgements, the less we account for them.

When Avicenna demonstrates *by* thought that it *is* thought accesses 'generality in forms', distinguishing categories, physics from metaphysics, genera or universals as against particulars, he justifies what is *seen* in physics by their metaphysic derivation from the 'form' of an *idea*. This firmly places things of physics as the short-lived expression of the *metaphysic being of something*.

This is authorised by the intelligible grasping that physics are derived and deducible from a metaphysic *truth of being*. *Substance* is ascertained more as an *essence*, a *being*, an abstraction, than a physical thing that is short-lived anyway, due to its physics within space and time. An apple cannot be what it is; a physical thing cannot be, not without the truth substance that underwrites it. We found this particularly in the case of the onion we considered earlier. This requires astute contemplation and judgement to be made. How much are we to tolerate the self-evidential true being of things that we encounter as sensible objects or objects of abstraction. Introspection and private meditation of this sort must link with our private interests.

The work of Ludwig Boltzmann largely centred on astute judgement, though himself often rejected by established science as a 'discomforter' of sorts. He disturbed received views. This was no less than many had done before him. His theorem said to prove an 'irreversible approach to equilibrium', with scrutiny of entropy, is suggestive of very much the *rest* to which I have alluded as an ultimate *position of motionlessness.* This has no affect at all on any substance of truth that may pertain, but it is a reasoned attempt to grasp it.

In the inevitable pursuit of this, he applied the anthropic principle to physics, (things having to be as they are in the interim *in order* to reach 'rest'). He admitted *unobservable theoretical entities* into his considerations, scientific heresy to his contemporaries, so supporting the notion of Bolzano before him of *theoretical definition*, and who in turn anticipated the later notions of *non-mental entities*. By this is meant the *being* of objects of truth as abstractions *beyond* observational potential.

The discomfort such theories offered to the established science community does not disqualify them as mere 'speculation', and as they are supported by self-consistent stages of well reasoned thought underpinning them they are difficult to dislodge. The interesting thing about such thinkers is that although dealing with *abstractions*, at times they disclose them through the language of mathematics and physics. This is less speculating than calculating.

Such calculating approach confronts any charge of speculation, one of the objections noted above, and as to the other, it is necessary to admit the broad spectrum of the *being of all objects of truth*, as each definable as an entity, however abstract or otherwise, or individuated as fragments of a greater 'whole'. This is closer to a grasp of the nature of truth, however incomplete for a comprehensive knowledge of it, than anything received wisdom would suggest. Had Pilate, Governor of Judea, had such apperception, he would not have needed to ask the philosophic question of Christ, 'what is truth?' Having grasp of it he would have remained as silent in the question as was Christ in his reply.

There is further objection made to *universals* by some philosophy as to their regard as 'entities' of abstraction, on the basis that were there no particulars in the sensory world, universals could not exist. If there were no white 'things' there could be no 'whiteness'. This is indeed so in the restricted sense of physics, but by close conversation with an astute blind man, it is found *not* to be so.

Without the blind man's reliance on the experience of many white 'things', he is yet still well able to envisage 'whiteness' that is *meaningful* to him. This is not so only of a man who *becomes* blind, but a man blind from birth. That he is not denied access to 'whiteness' can be explained, and without reliance upon sense objects with which he is not acquainted. The object of his contemplation is more 'solid', (in the Zeno sense), to him, than any object of pure speculation.

To explain it we find ourselves thrown back onto the view of Plato or Aristotle that 'whiteness' to the blind man has '*form*' although he has no *experience* of white 'things', *or* any observable particulars that are white. As we are dealing here also with 'imagery' and not words, issues of language are extraneous. *Something* presents to the blind man's mind, and, as we have seen, 'mind' is a threshold of *noumena* rather than phenomena. It bridges freely with the metaphysic principle engaging with objects of thought to which it moves.

As to the broad objection to universals as any sort of entity, there is more to any individual thing than its status as a particular. It is more than its properties and attributes. What these are relation to, for Plato, is conceptual *form*, and for Aristotle it is *essence*, while for me it is *truth*. This is the necessary substance of what *is*. Unless attributes and properties are *of a thing of truth*, an object in question cannot be anything. It must have true *being*, (substance), before attributes and qualities are accommodated.

Bertrand Russell is right to say that if all the properties are removed from a thing, there is nothing of the thing left. This is like the leaves peeled from an onion. What must be distinguished however is what there is nothing left *of*, and this is of course indisputably a *sense object*. It is the 'thing' of physics. The intelligible *object of truth* of the onion is nonetheless undisturbed or affected and remains the object to thought that always it is.

Though no *phenomena* may remain to be observed, the *truth object* is unaffected, and this is beyond physics under the metaphysic principle. Beyond the time the *sense object* of the onion *exists*, its *truth object abides*, and although stripping it of its leaves, (its properties and attributes), strips it also of its physical existence, they too are extensive as truth, but as applicable to a *truth object* of the sensory world. They are required to conjoin or relate to an *essential abstraction*. An onion is an intelligible truth object *as well as* a sensible one. So too are its attributes of independent leaves. I rest my own case there and feel no further explanation is necessary.

Virtues, which require us to reconcile with values, are not sensible objects, but intelligible ones, like the truth we considered at the beginning of this chapter, and, like the substance of the onion, its Platonic *form*, its Aristotelian *essence*, or *true being*, they are *abstractions*, though no less *real* for that. They are not found in a field or a pond, but are things of which there are consequences, often entailing events, in the sensory world. Acts of thought, intuition, and 'feelings', prevent them from being things of which we are ignorant, in spite of their immateriality.

Man does not compulsively *behave*, as animals do, but empowered by the force of intelligence and will, is at liberty to exercise preference and choice. In his epistemic privacy he must judge where it is he discerns some light, and by whatever means. The most natural impulse he has is to move to the light, (what is intelligible to him), to the good, to the benevolent, (notwithstanding that he sometimes also chooses to overrule this).

The degree of his insight and sensitivity is a component of his mindset. 'Moving to the light' brings him a sense of *freedom*, from private guilt, or public shame, and often brings with this, widespread acclaim by his fellows, even where this does not concern him in choices he makes. We have already considered the 'poles' of intended choice.

However man may be seen everywhere to be 'in chains' as Rousseau declares, the remark is not so rigid or fixed as it seems, remembering Wilde's contrary remark that 'stone walls do not a prison make'. Man's experience in *life and experience* may well bring the harshness or difficulty of chains or prisons, but his *being and spirit* easily provides sanctuary to him where he chooses, and that renders such chains spurious.

Historically this is apodeictic in the lives of many individuals and is a sure and certain indicator of our potential for transcending the harshness of the *physical* by embracing the *metaphysical*. This is no less than a 'trade-off' of what *passes* for what *abides*. Curtailment of our freedom has no purchase when we are already aloof from what obstructs it, and in our clinging to virtue, we are neither with guilt nor shame, but bathed only in the comfort of a light, not derived of sensible and passing things, but intelligible constants. This light, when we see it in others, is like that in a window, showing somebody is home. It is a sense of assurance. The spirit lives.

Though men prefer moving to the light, or clinging to virtue, rather than some poor substitute like ethics, it may not be possible. It may be that such an approach thrusts great fears upon them. Yet if man does not follow this instinctive light, it may disturb the delicate balance and harmony of his emotive and intellective peace with himself. As Jung notes, this may not only cause him anxiety, but may so disturb his unconscious as to lead to some neurosis, turning him at worst to depravity, crime, and sleepless nights. Whatever he says and does is required to be consistent with what he thinks. In such choices as where this is not so, the promise of light is abandoned.

Avoiding such a course promotes within man a sense of calm and tranquillity, a stable state of endurance and resignation that he is at pains not to abandon in the face of trial. This can only best be described also as a position of peace and rest. Meaning harm to none of his fellows, he is in a position of harmony both of his intellect and his emotion, such as is described by Thomas More. Doing always his best, he is aware also of what he cannot change, and this is largely the philosophic attitude of the Stoic, as so evident in the works of Marcus Aurelius, the benevolent emperor of Rome, who could be critical of the Roman policy of persecuting men for what they think, such as in the case of Christians.

It follows that what renders man most at peace and rest within, is his recognition of primary sort of what is *intelligible* to him, and greater, than what is merely sensible, which can never be more than a collection of incomplete 'things'. It is his intelligence places him at the threshold of the unexpected with confidence. He is empowered to engage with truth and realities, *not provided only by sense data* emitted by sensory objects, open to *perceiving*, but also by intelligible data from insistent abstract objects, of a non-material kind, engaging to his mind, and open to *conceiving*.

It may be contrived to avoid responsible account for abstractions, or abstract 'entities', such as by making demands for empirical verification of non-empirical things, which, itself, is absurd. No precast category confusion of this kind can be weighed against truth that professes only indifference to it. Primarily it is truth authorises everything anyway. It is *as* absurd in effect as a parking attendant applying inappropriate criteria in the legitimate case of a permit holder.

If Christianity is to offer any advance on the Stoic frame of mind, it is with the principle that besides doing none harm, it was additionally of interest to do men good. It is here we find the traditional virtues of the classical world of Greece and Rome, such as wisdom, courage, moderation or temperance, and justice, extended by those of more Christian innovation, such as hope, charity, and love.

What is shared however, by such clinging to virtue, is the reaching of ultimate good, so harmonizing our *life* with our *being*, and so making ourselves 'whole'. These virtues, with sequential values, are not 'mind dependent', and therefore untrue and unreal *without* 'mind' to access them, but exist *independently* of minds. What is clear is that minds are required to engage with them by what Russell calls an 'act of thinking', which is all can *be* in a mind. This act of thinking is directed *at* something, the virtues, which are not *in* the mind but elsewhere. As abstractions, their truth and reality is beyond the sensory, and the physical. They rest with the metaphysic principle.

The metaphysical principle is not a world, or a place, as I said earlier, for these are sensory terms concerning physics and motion. What is intelligible and abstract, true and real is inclusive to the principle, but as I said before, we do not have to fabricate an equivalent 'world' for this, as Plato does. It is, nonetheless, a principle gluing all true and real things. Plato recognises its integrity, calling it reality, (while inventing a 'world' to contain it), and the theologian refers to it as Paradise. However we image it, it is certainly not 'all in the mind' where there are no 'objects' or 'places', but merely acts of thinking 'bridging' with meaningful things.

Time measures change. We have I hope established that things of the sensory and physical world have no truth or reality unless they have *also* intelligibility, which in turn brings them *extension beyond* the merely sensory, and therefore the temporal. Further, we are well aware that things of the physical world must end, while things truly of the intelligible world *cannot*. It is reasonable to infer from this that when things, real and true *because* they are intelligible, decay or die, what they lose is physical *existence*, not their true and real *being*, which remains intelligible and unchangeable, as truth and reality, *always* beyond, and not governed by physics.

Absolute truth, and all unchangeable fragments of it, is constant, fixed, and fragments are the components or structure of what is traditionally referred to as the order of the 'logos'. We may think of it as the motherboard to anything that can rightly claim to 'be'. Always it is accessible to mind, and *conscience* is its authoritive or divine voice, heard within the individual. Even in the world of physics, intelligible form presents itself, and the mind taps into the 'motherboard' of truth for its provenance. The self-critical mental communicator with truth prompts the conscience; 'I've done something wrong and must fix it'. True being must surface. The divine voice consolidating truth mediates with the agent of the individual human spirit. The intelligibility principle is connecting divine authority with the free agent.

Ethics, like the sensible object in physics of the Cutty Sark, (and its planks and sails), are subject to change, while the good, virtue, or object of thought of the ship, is not. Things mind dependent, like ethics, have 'nowhere to go' even if they *could* be 'ongoing' for some other reason, for clearly they lack grounding in the basis of truth, as any variety of reality.

They are a contrived procedure of approaching *desired* things. Though clearly they may be *believed* as concepts, and even incorporated into laws, that in itself neither raises them to the validity status of virtues, nor carries the credentials of necessary truths. They are schemata of man's devising which may be true or false, while only what is both true *and* intelligible has ongoingness or durability. Ethics reduce to no more than opinion.

Such concepts as ethics may be, are assembled by agreed proposition, *perceived* as truth perhaps, but their fundamental weakness lies in the fact that always they are subject to change, and therefore time. A thing of truth and reality is intelligibly what it is only when it obtains unconditionally, and under *all* circumstances, but this cannot be claimed for ethics, as a way to validate them as a true and real code for conduct.

Ultimately and clearly, ethics are meaningless as any sort of eternal truth. In direct contrast, morality, or the implementation of *virtue*, and values so derived, are rigid, unchangeable, and obtain *always*, so having extension beyond the sensory world. Durability hallmarks truth. Extension is implied by durability while intelligibility assures perpetual meaning.

Virtues, and therefore values attendant upon them, are wholly independent of time and space, and clearly *other worldly* in provenance. As intelligible things, they have presence and place in the sensory world of living men, by the choices made and by words and actions among them, of *lasting* significance even beyond their physical lives. Times, lives, sensible things in the physical world, are ever in *motion,* while in the clinging to virtue, as chief contemplation in the mind, always there is accessible a place of *rest.* This is the secret of Stoic and Christian alike in establishing a quality of life wholly unperturbed by *any* event.

However *intelligible* a standard of correctness expressed by an ethic, may seem to qualify as plausible truth, as it ceases to *be* when minds thinking it cease, it no longer obtains, and, like an illusion, can only be something false, and merely *believed* to have true *being* while having none. The only ongoing truth to which it is justly entitled is that of *falsehood,* but this is *negation,* (or non-being), and it enters a paradox of contradiction that diverges from the notion of perpetuity and rest.

For the sake of clarity, truth may present in two differing ways. Either a necessary or required state of truth may arise, when 'this' and 'that' are so, establishing the state or condition of truth as evidential, and applicable to a thing, or the intelligible face-to-face presence of a thing is apprehendable *only* as truth by its self-evident *itness,* as in the case of a 'man being present'. The state or condition of truth may therefore present either as *evident* from supporting factors, or as *self-evident* by face-to-face encounter.

Passing time does not change the intrinsic *truth-substance* value of a thing, how much it is cherished for itself, and what it means to us, however much we may strive to ascribe some *other* kind of value to it, such as financial. A cabbage at the battle of Hastings in 1066 is the precise equivalent, no less and no more, in truth substance, to a cabbage today. By contrast, a farthing, or quarter of a penny in money, at the time of the battle has the equivalence of use today of ten pounds, and a penny that of forty pounds. We are obliged to conclude from this that the *substance value* of a cabbage then and now, has not changed a jot, while the penny has vastly changed. The cabbage has intrinsic value of meaning the same today as a thousand years ago, while money has no intrinsic *substance,* or true value at all. Money is merely an illusion declaring a *value we attribute* to it in relation to *other* things.

This has precise equivalence to the intrinsic substance values of virtues, that are changeless, and the synthetic values *we attribute* to an ethic, a politick, or money. Such objects of consideration as these are whimsical and unstable while virtue, to say the least at this point, is perennial. Charity has no substance of truth where it is merely *affected,* and simulated to achieve gain.

The particular of a cabbage, or a virtue, is resolutely rigid and fixed as an object of truth substance, in spite of one form of it presenting as a *sense object* while the other is an *object of abstraction*. Both, *as objects of truth*, (out of reach and beyond the control of physics), are changeless, and as such cannot therefore end, for this incurs change. When there is no change, time is irrelevant. They are each truth entities, (however fragmentary from the whole of true things). Instants of encounter between Harold and the sense object intelligible to him, the cabbage, are at once all events of truth to minds, (they are intelligible), and forever must be so. As sense objects however, both Harold and his cabbage are *also* in motion, which must end in entropy. As objects of truth, both remain. The truth of Harold, *and* his cabbage, is there, even when *they*, in any context of physics, are not. This is why any tragedy, as earlier quoted, is never less by the passage of time.

It is intelligible truth empowers us to refer to either of them, in terms of *universals*, or objects of abstraction. Cabbages profess *cabbage-ness*; individuals profess *man-ness*, and virtues profess *virtueness*. Universals are our way by thought of bridging with unending truths, only because they have true being as abstractions that abide always. Universals do not convey individual cabbages and virtues, but convey the objects of truth *substance*, or *essence*, underpinning individual things, albeit of differing categories. We are perfectly able to image individuals by *personalising* them with our own creative imagery, (as we may indeed do with Harold *and* his cabbage), but only because they have the truth substance to which we may add properties of choice.

So what we claim does not mean that a cabbage King Harold's cook plucked for the king's supper should therefore still *exist* because it is a *truth object*. That particular sense object was in the command of physics, and *ending* as a sense object is the rule within the order of physics. *Existing* terminates, *being truth* does not. What the king ate was the *sensible object of a cabbage*, not its substance or essence as *truth object*. This could not satisfy his hunger at all. As object of truth it remains. It is the phenomenon he consumed and not its abstraction, remaining firmly embedded as a truth object in metaphysics always, so that we access it as a noumenal object to thought, long after the event, and at this moment of passing time a thousand years later.

In effect, King Harold's cabbage is a *sensible object of truth in physics*, (phenomenon), while simultaneously it is a non-sensory *object of truth in metaphysics*, (a noumenal abstraction). When physically present, clearly it is an object of both, but when no longer physically present, it retains *being* as a noumenal abstraction. It is this truth substance that informed it as a sense object or cabbage.

Established sensible physical objects that are intelligible are truth objects by substance or essence, as truths, remaining noumenally accessible independently of whether or not they present as phenomena. Objects of truth entirely noumenal, with *no* attached phenomena, so long as they are intelligible by astute reasoning procedures, etc., can *also be known*, though as earlier we showed, they do not *require* to be known to *be* truth objects. We do not now know our unborn child, perhaps, but if he is to exist, already he is truth of which we are unaware.

The truth object of a particular individual cabbage is bound in perpetuity as an object, to truth, (the 'heimat' of its substance), and, it is obliged thereby to *outlast* any physical properties it may display in the physical world. Long after the observable cabbage decays in time and space, its truth object, (substance or essence), adamantly remains as a truth object upon which acts of thinking may be directed. For the reaching of such objects of abstraction, with no physical presence, it is mental vitalism that is required. There is no sense data available but there is intelligible data of another order relying only on truth that is intelligible to us by the act of thinking, (conceiving), and not on any act of seeing or touching, (perceiving).

Whether a truth is the necessary outcome of reasoning, a realizable *condition* of something, and noumenal, or whether we are face to face with an itness of identity, a phenomenon, truth is the foundation of its actuality, and this so whether or not the object contemplated is physical or an abstraction. Without conditional, or self-evident truth, there can be no actuality or purchase on reality. Once the condition of truth is satisfied, by reasoned thought for example, (and as truth does not change or end), actual presence of physical order, is simply not required as further evidence.

By these means it is with some ease that we are empowered to distinguish between a virtue and an ethic, between a descriptive narrative and a fiction, between an apparition and an illusion, and between *life and existence*, on one hand, and the extensive *being* of truth, on another, typical of that conjoining and composing the state of the human individual.

Of course this necessitates wilful *upgrading* of an object we contemplate, from the strictly sensory and corporeal contemplative world, in terms of *perception*, to the mental command of what can be contemplated, in terms of *conception*. Our consciousness is then required to negotiate with what is ascertainable *only* by thought, and however reasonable an approach engaged, with no sense data to support it, many *reject* objects of contemplation of a non-material sort. If we recognise our fellows as walking spirits, and therefore everlasting, rather than merely disposable units of flesh, it is certain that we cannot treat them unjustly. Although sense data is entirely redundant to this awareness, many are so habitually dependent upon it as to reject the whole metaphysic principle, which is absurd.

In my final chapter to follow, I continue my quest to establish the clear distinction between the physical and the spiritual, the sensory and non-sensory, existence and being, as interlocking features of all private human life and experience. No human individual is complete in his experience without engagement between what is seen and what is thought. Acts of thinking, (what is conceived), are as indispensable as are all that is perceived. Man is poised always between motion, (physics), and rest or peace, (metaphysics), and unless responsive to both, is incomplete and unrealised.

Chapter 10 – Man as Immaterial Entity

We know what we are but cannot see what we be.

(Inspired by Ophelia)

We see our bodies daily as we go about conscious life and existence, and understand that neither our ancestors nor ourselves is what energises them, in spite of genetic inheritance. What we inherit genetically is very like a printed circuit, unexercised or unplugged from any source of power, and, therefore, potential but unresolved. Like the shadow of Jung, *something* does energise this baseboard, (occasionally revealing its presence in our unconscious), however amorphous. In Priestley's mirror we are aware of this something *other* that is not physical yet bound in intimate relation to us.

It is in this connection and at this point, where we have attributed to physical sensible objects, and to objects of abstraction alike, proportionate participation, (or contribution), to a total summation of some complete reality fabric, that now we need to address the issue of whether any sort of ongoing durability may be expected of any sensible object of which there are *instances* in the world.

Reasoning of such a possibility draws much support and inspiration from many sources, not only in general from an abundance of Western philosophy that is in league with Christian thought, but also in particular from philosophic sources without this commitment. Making connections between Classical thought, such as that of Plato, Aristotle, Parmenides, and on through Hegel to Gabriel Marcel, it is possible to filter a near consensus view or philosophic attitude.

Though it cannot be claimed, while living and conscious, and therefore very reliant on sense data from physical 'things', that we can wholly understand, by the usual criteria we apply to what can be *knowable*, an actual realityscape that we cannot perceive, we are sufficiently endowed to ascertain and conceive something of its nature. To do so however, requires that we deal with abstract entities offering no sense data, especially in view of the fact that, as already indicated, any *actual*, (however unperceivable), realityscape is presupposed to be inclusive of them.

The aim of preceding chapters has been to uncover a reality sustained, and underwritten by a foundation and superstructure composed of fragmentary yet required objects of truth. These are primarily intelligible, and therefore accessible to mental vitalism, and thereby through life. They are objects of truth necessary and required to add to the wholeness and completeness of reality, (requiring them to be what they are), while individually only fragments, and intelligible as 'parts' of an order (the complete reality). They have actual connections and presence in relation to thought and mind.

Such fragmentation of objects of truth allowing us to recognise them individually, is created by their 'spontaneous act of liberty', (Schelling's expression applies when we single them out *as* objects of worth or value). Nonetheless, no one of them encapsulates all of reality. Separate from the whole of it, they still are only fragments of it. For example, one cannot wholly be virtuous by being justified to claim the virtue of temperance, if that is all can be said. Each unit or fragment like this is a contingent only of the whole fabric of virtue in general. Though not to be confused with the 'monad' of Leibniz, which he uses differently anyway, individuated objects of truth are units, albeit *like* the monad, combining into complete reality. We may picture them as the individual cells, each of which are in required assembly to comprise a whole beehive.

In such a complex there is no way we can know every cell of the hive, and no way either then that we can know the whole hive, (or the whole of reality). We cannot be familiar with every cell, but readily recognise that however many there may be, we can be sure that there is a sum *total* of them. Whatever this complete total may be is the *whole*. In the same way are we obliged to recognise that however the sum is composed, there *is* a whole of all true things. (The 'one' of the ancients).

We recognise also and in addition to this, that certain cells of which we do have knowledge, have affinities with others so forming kinship in groups, and then we apprehend classes or categories of cells, or objects of truth. Each category or class is distinct from another. Yet even one group that may contain many cells, cannot encapsulate the whole, but must be added to all other groups for the 'whole' to be realised.

Self evident and distinct groups, classes, or categories, like this, in terms of being *most* obvious, that throughout life and experience men *cannot* evade, are ubiquitous, and at the head of any descending hierarchy, or order of subordinate classes that may follow, are the quite distinct orders of objects of truth that we describe as physics *and* metaphysics. Again, neither alone captures the whole realityscape, for without physics, metaphysics cannot be intelligible when there is no thought brain or mind, and without metaphysics, there can be no true or real *significance*, for nothing of physics alone is *unchanging* or escapes degeneration, and cannot therefore conform to truth alone.

This presents as something unarguable, rightly putting any demeaning of metaphysics into some stagnant intellective pool. As indicated earlier, immaterial objects of truth will *not* be ignored in daily life and experience, and it would be impossible without them. Without metaphysic substance of truth men are no more real than the fairies at the bottom of an enchanted garden.

We understand at a profound level, and especially in private contemplation, that we have no *fictional* integrity, and that indeed we have true being of *some* lasting significance to *some* order of things. What we have lasting significance *to* is the order of the whole of all things. What is real must be of truth, and what is of truth is reality.

As this order is unchangeable, as truth, the thing to which we have such intimate relation is at liberty to pertain *without* dependence upon the bodies in which we find ourselves *for a time.* They have insufficient durability to qualify, alone, as an entity of truth. This serves as a major breech in holding belief only in what is experienced in the realm of physics. We are obliged to engage simultaneously with a *different* order of experience, *beyond* our bodies, with what can be ascertained reasonably by thought. The metaphysic principle is unavoidable by the searching mind.

Leibniz brings important support to such a notion when he claims that '*matter and motion are not so much substances or things as they are the phenomena of percipient beings*', and he places the reality of these in the context of a governing harmony. This is reminiscent of our 'sigma', 'logos', or whole of all things of truth. Experience of a physical order of things *in time and space* is incomplete without experiencing also, by thought, the unfolding of their relation to *truth.* What is left to a man other than despair when his incomplete order of experience is limited in relation only to *matter and motion*?

Where we find ourselves in a material world is like the scientist's understanding of 'present encounters'. We may first encounter a block of ice, but if it were heated we would then find water, and if the water should become heated our first encounter could just as easily be a gas or steam. Depending on the *instant* of our arrival in time and space, we can encounter any of the changing states of the same 'thing', so that encountering changed states and transition is the rule to human life and experience. It is a material scenario to which we are exposed. Differing centuries expose men to differing states of affairs, but this does not make men different species.

Like all participants in a material world, the human body conforms to the laws of physics and transition, place and time, but it does not do so alone. It is twinned with, or entails, an impartial observer, an assessor, an adjudicator, appraising its progress interestedly, urging adherence to objective standards, (like the virtues), sometimes inconvenient to the body's appetites. This arbiter is most apparent when the conscience imposes expectations, when guilt or shame are experienced, or at times of inspired creativity, or times of the apprehension of what can be life-changing insights. What is entailed in directions, taken submissively by the body, is the mental life and vitality of *mind*.

It is quite unnecessary to instruct any individual on the very real and true dynamic and vitalism of this constant presence of *mind*, or the submissive attitude of the body to its imperatives, (and even the body's rebellion against them). The true being of an immaterial *mental life* is universally acknowledged in epistemic privacy, which induces men to feel there is something greater within them than their bodies alone. Priestley's observation concerning the mirror makes very plain *the incompleteness of what is seen*.

Yet Gilbert Ryle supposes it a category mistake to ascribe to mental life *actual* metaphysical significance. He attributes to it only the skill of the illusionist. Such a supposition cannot withstand scrutiny for numerous reasons, especially as the assertion itself is dismissive of a *self-evident* category, (that of metaphysics), anyway. Even he cannot deny the *function* of mind in the ways I have presented to this point, and does not so do, but in the manner of some neurological scientists, he is relying on this function as merely the derivative outcome of particular conditions of physics with regard to the brain. This is an attempt to claw back significance and meaning to the realm of physics, so to avoid altogether the actual abstract entities of metaphysics.

This reduces the order of human life to the material significance zone of mere *behaviourism* as the result of mechanisms of physics. While this may well be sufficient to the leading of a brutish animal life programmed in much the same way as a machine, so that everything is reduced to physical biology, it is a theory insufficient to explain the very *actual* encounter of free will. Without this no action could be freely self-determining or carry self-responsibility.

In addition, it erases *evident and actual* motivation for self-improvement or advance, regardless of the sometime hardship this involves, and beyond what serves immediate appetites, (even endorsing these, of whatever kind). It denies the significance of universal and *actual* acknowledgement of there being any objective criteria, such as are the virtues, *actually* accessible to mind, sufficient to influence codes of behaviour. We have evidence of the *actuality* of significant things unseen, ubiquitous to mental life, yet of import beyond any reach of brain mechanisms normally dependent on appetite, physics, or a body's needs; things that only the metaphysical principle can compass. Ryle's theory is a 'horse that will not run'.

The twin of human identity, *itness*, the mental life energising and animating the body, is not the same category or order of the body, as a thing of physics. It is the human *being of truth*, beyond the cell of physics where the *body* is obliged to reside, and of which there could be nothing, *but* for the basic requirement that *if* untrue, it could not exist. While still living and experiencing it is a constant companion often revealing itself in the unconscious. It is the *percipient being*, of which Leibniz speaks, making intelligible the phenomena it encounters, and the interaction between 'things' and the human individual, and between one being and another of fellow men.

If Ryle and his mechanisms were right, such interaction could be to no purpose other than serving private indiscriminate appetite triggered in the absence of will. Whether good or evil, there would be no responsible choice of authentic private action, and we would merely respond to chemical impulse. This scenario of meaningless abandonment and bankruptcy of individual worth is wholly rejected by the very *evident* actuality and utility of the metaphysic principle in our dependence on abstractions, and the well received order of a logos.

When questioned as to the true identity and significance to any man, and of what can be understood as beginnings and endings, in the context of *existing*, or *being*, or how physics and metaphysics can be synchronous, (while we live and experience), the founder of Christianity elects a two-fold complex as an aid for us to grasp what composes a *duplexity*.

This duplex scenario can be demonstrated by a folding rule, where two parallel arms of a folding rule carry separate if related pieces of information, distinguishable from each other, yet composing *one* single object and matrix. One part companions the other. The one part is incomplete to the whole. This illustrates both what is seen *and* what is ascertained or gathered of any human individual, for the whole rule is not observed at once, but a part at a time. Studying one part of the scale does not leave us unaware of the other. Man also is a two-fold complex. Christ mentions Himself how a cup requires not merely its outer boundary, but an inside space, also. There is singularity and *whole* identity to a two-fold complex in many things, as in the duality of man, and as supported by Descartes, as the two-sided coin demonstrates.

Things of the sensory world, sensible 'things' are *never* at rest, but always in motion, or as Heraclitus calls it, in 'flux'. However, if not false, and they are true *and* intelligible, they cannot become untrue or unintelligible, but must obtain *always*. The sensible form of an apple, which Caesar eats, must, in the physical world, change, but its intelligible counterform, when the apple is 'no longer' physically present, in substance or essence, and in its associated attributes and qualities, must obtain *always* as a thing of truth.

Whatever we do with the sensible object of the Cutty Sark, its intelligible counterform always applies. We are empowered, whenever we may choose, to contemplate its object to thought, as in the latest case, an apple, which once also presented in the physical world to Caesar, though the consuming of it in the physical world erases its *life* or existence in the world. This has no affect whatever on its true *being* as an intelligible object, encountered by Caesar. Caesar really *did* eat a *real* apple of *dual* capacity. Something with both *life and existence* and *truth being*.

'No longer' is a meaningless description of any intelligible *being*, for the expression applies to *sensible things in motion*, and not things *complete and at rest*. Once at rest they are devoid of physical presence and there can be no instance of them in the sensible world. As an object of intelligible truth, the apple concerned extends *always* and beyond the sensible object, which no longer *exists*, for the physical apple is neither its *essence* or *truth substance*. This cannot submit to the entropy of physics or *end*.

Completion and rest is the state of resolved being, essence and substance, liberated from motion, and in perpetual calm. There can be no way of verifying this in a sensory world of confinement, where *all* things are in motion, and things routinely cease to *exist*, and where all verification procedures naturally require factors of physics to establish *anything* observed of an object contemplated. That direction of inquiry leaves us with the implication that only a thing of physics *can* reliably be verified, (the *sensible object* of apple or onion as against its *intelligible one*).

The erroneous inference readily developed from this is that *existence is all that defines being* while the fact remains that being truth and existing are quite distinct things. The two are confused. Existence by tactile presence, or memory of it, as a particular, is all that is contemplated or considered credible when trapped by such mindset. One entity *being a feature of truth* while simultaneously *experiencing life* is ignored.

We have here a closed system of physics, following its direction of time to entropy, applied to two distinct things, leaving no exigency for truth being fixed and rigid, so *requiring* completion *by* extension. In addition to this as clearly something comes to an end, it cannot be this unchanging truth, or any sort of reality. 'It was never really anything!

This tends to diminish inference, however well supported, of the *truth being* of anything extending *beyond* its physics. In this inappropriateness of evaluation by means of physics or any procedure of material verification, the sole avenue open for our evaluation is that of self-consistent thought in reasoning procedures. Ultimate resort to the metaphysic principle is therefore unavoidable. Reliance on the sensible object or a particular of physics in its closed system, as any truth or reality, is then redundant. Objects of truth, closed to the senses, are revealed by acts of thinking, and for this, mental life is *necessary*.

It is mental vitalism we employ when considering that Caesar may have had an aversion or allergy for apples, or never ate one, and it is even a remote possibility that he never encountered one. We are, however, obliged to confront whether or not this is *likely*. Certainly we must agree that he was indeed likely to be familiar with apples, and, at least on one occasion was likely to have eaten one. Only one conclusion of any sensible sort can be made from all of this, and on the basis, not of proof, (which is impossible), but by means of a *probabilist* procedure, (not to be confused with 'probability' to which probabilist *procedure* leads), and probabilism leads us to conclude that it is a likely *truth* that Caesar ate an apple on *some* occasion. This is a *judgement* of profound importance. After all, when he ate it we were not there. We encounter a very likely truth *being* without our observing it, a feature of mental life

What is profound about it is that it is a *judgement* that is capable of assessing a likely being of truth without having to rely on any physical evidence of the event. It can raise its profile as something *knowable* by probability. Without any documentary or historic aid of recorded evidence, and inferring something as a likely truth by reasoning procedure alone, sufficiently supports the judgement subsequently made. It is persuasively knowable as a truth even if not guaranteed.

Probabilism is at the heart of many creditable theories, offering worthy propositions later confirmed, and is central to much philosophical thought, as with Thomas Aquinas, the Atomists of Greece, (though deprived of the technology to apply what they thought), and Boltzmann a century ago with his consideration of a 'timeless order in physics'.

All we have as purported evidence amounts to no more than a 'statistical likelihood'. Yet it seems we have sufficient confidence to judge that Caesar *must* have eaten an apple at some time, and we conclude this to be a *likely* truth. It is a theory of a likely truth scenario as against what is *unlikely*, such as Caesar being unfamiliar with apples, which we have ruled out. As in the case of all theories, this is the best we can do, though conclusions so drawn carry a notable degree of convincing authority.

Without the enormous input of truth in the business of physical existence and life, there could be nothing at all. Truth may be perceived, conceived, pursued, appraised, or denied, but in spite of being an abstraction, as an agent, (and maybe more), of the metaphysic principle, it remains always fixed and rigid. Clearly it precedes and succeeds all that can lay claim to *being* at all, whether physical or abstract, and regardless of time. It is before things, during things, and after things, over-riding time, so that something truly is, was, or will be. Such descriptions of tense are things *of* time and space relevant only to physics and time. Remove truth, *of being,* from any of them and there is nothing to be 'timed' by *any* of them.

The metaphysical principle provides no detailed explanation of many things we may encounter; but it does underwrite the *truth* of them *as* they become intelligible. Something may present to us for which we have no ready explanation, such as the reliable report of a sighting of a ghost, and the assertion of the truth of its 'presenting' underpins the event without offering one. What is missing here is reliable and objective judgement such as to make the ghost intelligible and thereby a truth.

While an actual presentation of a ghost requires explanation if it is to be *known* as a truth, its deficiency as being readily explained is denied by the absence of any other sense data than that alone of *appearance.* Yet at the same time, the truth of this appearance may be so persuasive by impassioned testimony as to suggest the truth of it. That ghosts are universally encountered does *seem* to suggest the truth of them, where there is sufficient credible testimony to suggest it, but there would seem little sense data available in relation to physics by which such experiences may be regarded seriously. However persuasive by reputable source, even as in the case of Carl Jung, the eminent psychiatrist, we are left to conclude that we cannot *know* that ghosts, (or spirits in his case), have any true being. This does not mean however that they are *not* a truth.

Nonetheless, and in spite of insufficient evidence by any means of physics, and however disconcerting this may be, metaphysics underwrites the true being of many things we are obliged to take into account. Without this, authentic things, as *objects* of truth, disregarding of any sense data being available, from beauty through virtue to triangles, could not pertain. However persuasive we may be, for example, with the victim of such an encounter with a ghost, where sincerely held, we are unlikely to remove his *fear* of ghosts, (as one philosopher suggests), so that for him it must remain a credible object of truth to contemplate.

If we have no sense data on beauty, virtue, and triangles, as universals of verity, (only particular examples or aspects of them), yet are prepared to find them entirely credible, to what purpose should we regard ghosts differently. It is our firm knowledge of them in the zone of physics that is denied us, not their seldom-observed, (if ever accredited), truth of being. After all, this is the *object of being* to which those fearful *acts of thinking* in minds are directed, especially when unmotivated by creative imagination.

Intelligibility as *objects of truth*, granted to the appearances of ghosts is clearly not sponsored by any imaginative projection when, as in the similar experience of predictive dreams, such an appearance is strengthened as intelligible by some historic fact or facts, uncovered to support an apparition's credibility. The credentials of predictive dreams and wandering spirits being supported by earlier or later events and historic record, provides such intelligibility as the metaphysic principle certainly underwrites.

Emphasising the primary requirement of metaphysic *truth-being* as underpinning all things, even motion and physics *itself* emerges from a point of *rest*, (where there is no physics). We are led by science to accept that at some second point of 'singularity' it is to such rest that ultimately it must return. It follows that physics lie in the commanding palm of metaphysics *always*, (the realm of *truth-being*, whether or not they *exist*, or for whatever period, and independently), for certainly they are a truth. Many things of physics, like many truths, and like the viability of ghosts, are not required to be *known*. Truth of *being* does not require to be *known*; yet it is *knowable* on occasion.

This is what distinguishes the dynamic of physics, 'slumming in a basement', where the dynamic is *motion*, the 'engine' of physics, from the *truth* of physics. It is truth that is the metaphysic dispenser of authenticity and credentials, (giving potential *being*), *to* basement, dynamic, *and* engine. *Origination* is clearly not a matter of physics. The origination of a human individual relies on the credentials and authenticity of true *being*, bestowed under the metaphysic principle, if ever it is to be meaningful and real.

If the scenario of human individual lives has no significance or reality, other than the brute scenario of an ignominious 'end', as materialism may suggest, (like our engine of physics above), then no individual life can be taken seriously as anything true or real. We have a scenario without the symmetry of an equation. There is a huge omission, in that true being is altogether ignored. It simply suggests a frantic leaping from some biochemical phase of change to another, measured by time for however long *time* proceeds. We are left with the pure mechanism of a biological variety.

Physics themselves must be understood here to derive provenance and subsistence, in origination, as *truth-derived*, derivative of whatever motivated their inception; at that point of singularity we call the 'big bang'. Otherwise they could hold no credibility. Physics clearly are not self-standing but *caused*, as are their cohorts of space and time. Physics does not encapsulate truth, but is encapsulated *by* it, and qualifies as an abstraction from the whole of what *is*. They are thus, alone, an insufficient arbiter of reality.

If thought, abstraction, truth, the metaphysic principle, are put aside in favour of empirical physics and motion, then too must be dismissed any sense of evolutionary order in the cosmos, all mathematical projections, and calculable expectations. These rely entirely on *reasoned* truths and relations dealing in *abstract entities*. None of this is *physiocentric*. They allude to order of intellective nature that pre-exists man's grasping of them by intensive reflection.

The physiocentric, what concerns life and experience, is a thing private acquaintance and credible report lead us to suppose to be recognisable truth. This recognition is a form of knowing so that we may have no doubt of it. It is observed, and not mere opinion or belief that we hold without support. However, truth is unalterable, does not change, and has no end. *Always* it is truth. *This is knowable too*. It cannot become falsehood or *not* a truth. Yet simultaneously we are obliged to agree that life *is* finite and that it *ends*. This is an absurd conundrum, for truth must abide *always*, while the life (we presuppose instinctively to be truth) ends. There is however one single route of escape.

What is observed of human life within the laws of physics determinately ends. This is unarguable. Something that does *not* end must additionally be inclusive to this life of physics if it is to contravene its laws of disemblement en route to entropy, and qualify as unending truth or reality. Clearly what *is* additional cannot be itself subject to the laws of physics, if there is to be any sort of *truth* of a given human life, and if it is to abide always. This 'something' is obliged to be something independent altogether of physics. Generally we seem familiar with this and we refer to it as 'spirit', and the life of mind would seem to liaise with this, or to consist of it.

Truth is itself an abstraction, and not a physical 'thing', yet we find that any sort of life and its experiences is wholly dependent on it's pertaining as the underwriter of what *is*, or the precluder of what *cannot be*. This abstraction is therefore the authenticity and credentials of *anything* qualified to claim ongoing *being*, or always pertaining. Furthermore, this abstraction is wholly unaffected by the laws of physics, granting truth-being to *any* object of reality, (or what *is*).

While we experience and we live, it is perfectly possible for this 'brute fact' to be apprehended by thought and reasoning, (as demonstrated by Descartes), for *this* is an *experience of thought* that is the 'percipience' referred to earlier. Some may call it revelation, but it may just as easily be reasoned. *Beings of truth* are clearly beyond the affects of any laws of physics, even while represented *by* them within space and time.

This truth-being we consider here is an *endorsement* of the abiding reality, the non-material substance, essence, or being that *informs* human life within physics, but is always an *abstraction* of truth. Physics are themselves dependent on this same principle. Metaphysics carry none of the issues of physics and are not commanded by them. Whether it is the *reality* of human life and experience we contemplate, or the obligation to apprehend the abstraction of truth as instrumental in all we think and do, the metaphysic principle is very evident as a 'forced issue' that we must recognise, for all truth is compassed and authenticated by it.

Without truth there can be no reality, and all things are illusory. The only clear and confident judgement to be made from the viewpoint of physics *without* the metaphysic principle is the doubtless falsehood and unreality of *all* things, as objects of thing *or* objects of thought. There is nothing at all, and we are all figments of a demon's dream. There is neither *itness* alterity, nor other things, nothing *true*. Though we may imagine there is much pottery in the window, there is sadly no potter. This is not only unlikely, but also quite absurd. Truth, with all its abstractions, is *necessary*.

Without the truth of a thing nothing can be said to have *begun*, there is no possibility that *anything* can be other than a 'non-event'. It is redundant then to ask whether physical things are *finite* when they have no true being. They never truly 'are' at any time so that they cannot endure either, or be *infinite*. Yet we are saved from this in that *truth* is unalterable, unchangeable, and perpetual, and that it is an *abstraction* of reality. Physics and motion as a closed system *require* an end. The end of things of physic *is* truth, (an unending tenet of metaphysic import).

The missing factor necessary, whether we consider finite things or otherwise, is that of a *position of rest*. This position is one of true being. The implication of this indeed, is that all things in motion *must* ultimately reach *some* position of rest. It is a position of determination, allowing viability, as a bye-product, even to *sensible* things in motion, justifying how sensible things *truly* live or exist *by* coming to a sensory end. They could not otherwise be true 'things' proceeding to entropy, as they must, identifiable as sensible objects, and in submission to physical laws. It is their *truth* informs their existence, and it is their truth prevails.

That position of rest is the sure and certain end, when physical, not of its *substance of truth*, but of its animating physics in motion, (properties and attributes *of* the essence or substance that are physical), so that flux and motion reaches a threshold of *motionlessness*. Rest, however, is irreducible, unchangeable, and is simply what it is, and it does not admit motion, nor go away anywhere. Any 'thing', which proceeds through motion, ultimately *must* reach rest, but *no further*.

This demonstrates how even things of physics must resolve as truth whether by physical properties or metaphysic substance. A man's life resolves ultimately as an object of truth, and this an abstraction of perpetual being, inseparable from its required substance of truth. The 'always' *being* of truth, survives death, as it must because it is truth, and abides beyond it. This is what we recognise as the spirit of being, penetrating physics, to what lies beyond where there is quantifiable being *of* truth, but without motion. It is the condition of being truth. Thousands of years before Christ, and through the time of the Orphics, this was regarded as the truth object of a *soul*. Man, it was claimed, is both 'earthly' and 'divine'. He is body *and* soul.

In this regard, and returning to King Harold's cabbage for a moment, we demonstrated its 'ongoingness' or durability, beyond any time of its demise in physics, as an object of truth. While it is so, and that in spite of physics destroying the *sense object*, in degeneration, the *truth object* of the cabbage always continues to abide, this does not dispense to the cabbage the distinction of having a soul.

While a cabbage and a man share eternal significance as objects of true being, only man has the advantage of *mind*, with all that entails, providing him with the distinction that in all he encounters, whether tactile and physical, or contemplative and abstract, everything is *intelligible to him*. His will and self-determination make him thereby *accountable and responsible* in his application to ultimate justice, (the sufficient coming to rest of things), so that final resolution is open to him only by such portal and threshold that *soul* provides.

As it is with great ease that *mind* engages with non-sensory things, often things with which the body *cannot* engage, this is often how we come to associate mind and soul as holding some close relation. As what is concerned here is at the threshold of metaphysic being, (beyond reach of physics), verification by means of physics is never a possibility. We are not dealing exclusively with sense objects, so we may entertain little hope of identifying both mind and soul as one and the same thing. What we can be sure of however, with just a little rumination, is that at the very least, one or other would seem reasonably to be *required*, should they *not* be identical, for such extension and durability *beyond* physics, sufficiently to meet the requirements of perpetual truth.

For some, this may provide sufficient grounds for belief that they are indeed one and the same; that *mind and soul are one*, or what we mean by *spirit*. As mind is the bridge between physical and metaphysical things of abstraction, sensitising us *to them*, (as when we associate beautiful *things* with *beauty*), this is a truth of the human condition. We are sensitised to objects of abstraction by *mind*.

The archetype of beauty, and the mind in liaison with it, clearly is not a truth supportable by physic, but by metaphysic. As truth is changeless, it would seem at least *unlikely* that either beauty or the minds that liaise with it, should reach comprehensive *ending* of some kind, as when brain death is reached. *Extension of some kind*, beyond such a point in physics confining men to a suggestive full stop of death, (and although it cannot be verified by any *procedure* of physics), is a perfectly *reasonable* expectation. Such expectation is bedrock of Christian philosophy, while making sense of Priestley's experience of the mirror.

In addition to this, it is clear that we can distinguish brain from mind. The brain has unadulterated purchase on the world of physics and the sensory, whilst mind has access to wholly unphysical, or metaphysical, abstract objects of truth, even in the circumstances of brain malfunction. As Milton claims, the 'mind is its own place'.

What engages brains and minds at the onset of death often thereby differs, so that while things may disturb a brain, the clear and resolved mind of the one identity, may completely retain its composure. They are not of the same order. *The comfort of a resolved and authentic mind is indispensable.* Brain function, or dysfunction, for that matter, is something of inferior order, and if relevant at all resembles the stoker of a furnace, the warmth of which is something we feel.

Nonetheless, the significance of the brain cannot be dismissed, as it is the 'caretaker of life and existence'. The brain may be considered the assembly line of material to which the mind is a discriminating client.

The notion of duality, (body and mind or body and soul), from early history, carries with it a reduced and simple understanding of plain common sense. While things in motion obey physical laws, (as do material bodies, and brains for that matter), so that we witness their beginning and their ending, no metaphysical thing, (that is object of truth, *beyond* the control of physics, such as mind and spirit), can be expected to follow the same *command* of physics. Even physical things ultimately are commanded by the metaphysic principle. Man's mind is the mediator of what is intelligible.

When the sense data of any thing, be it boulder, ship, building, or human individual, is no longer, (time), emitted by the *thing in motion*, under the command of physics, and therefore physically not evident, it is clear that all motion has expended itself, and the 'thing' is subsequently motionless or *at rest*. It has stopped. The 'thing' has not gone *anywhere*, however, (this is a geophysical descriptive term), simply on the grounds that it has no evident physical properties, and because we cannot see it, touch it, or talk to it. All of these things derive of physics, none of which are evident from a position of rest or entropy. They are indeed, *physical* relations to *physical* things, and cannot be applied where there is no motion or physics, as for example, to *truths*.

Any motionless sensible entity attaining rest reaches *pleonasm*, (or diffuseness), shedding physical properties required for motion, which are redundant. We can say reliably that the entity no longer *exists*. It is not *in a place* or *at a time*, albeit it remains a truth. On these grounds alone however, what we *cannot* say, is that the entity signifies *nothing*, that we cannot *contemplate* it as an object to thought, or that there is no *object* of thought available upon which we could subsequently direct our *acts of thinking*, or about which we can ably speak. Our feelings towards such things do not end for they are not, in truth, ended. As object of truth being, it *cannot* end.

Rather than *nothing* then, such an entity is *something* even *without* its physical existence. It is evidently something of *intelligible* substance without any physical support. Clearly it is a true and durable entity of some sort of *being* for it continues to obtain *after* its life or existence. Equally clearly it has extension beyond physics, which we can only describe as something *metaphysical*, remote from fingertips, but imperative to *minds*, and minds are obliged to engage with what is seen *and* unseen in the order of everything. The same metaphysic principle informing our daily life and experience *beyond* what is seen, again asserts itself, and enforces its commanding authority revealing *the abiding of mind*.

This of course also converges with Christian philosophy with which it is entirely consistent. 'Death is nothing to fear for life is eternal'. In this regard, and in view of the direction of the theme of this book, it is interesting to note how two thousand years ago, when Christ was challenged as to the 'beginning' and 'ending' of things, and what this should signify to us, he gave the *overview* response that in life we are 'two in one', and that it was all a matter of *'motion and rest'*.

In motion we are thrust in *living* from one time and place to another, while in rest we are forever *being* in the sheltering aurora of spiritual and perpetual calm. This is a spiritual *eudaimonia* of intelligible well-being. Even while in motion we may bring a taste of such equanimity and enhancement to our lives, and the appendices to follow subscribe to this.

EPILOGUE

Lives are episodes of sense experience while the true being of their substance abides forever.

Precisely as North American Indian philosophy apprehended that the white man destroys 'mother earth', (blowing holes in the ground etc.), the very place on which he is dependent for his life and existence, we have come to understand the earth's natural resources approach total depletion.

Oil, until now a lubricant for the tectonic plates in the earth's crust, is being drained dry, while oxygen producing forests are routinely decimated. All such actions proceed by motion and physics to their predicable and natural terminus, *entropy*. As matter is persistently converted to energy, biological life becomes less tenable. In any race between the sun burning off its hydrogen, and man converting the earth's material to energy, it seems likely for man to be the winner in terms of the time necessary. Long before the sun reaches entropy, the earth should well have arrived.

This 'brute fact' is a predictable 'truth', possible and thinkable *before* it occurs, but continuing as an intelligible truth forever *always after* any such event. The substance of the event, physical in nature, in *truth being* can never change or end. What will remain of human individuals is the same being of truth, without any necessary physical evidence of any erstwhile human physical presence; *something simply not required to be truth.* The *essence*, or true being of men, therefore, must abide.

In contemplating how we may appreciate the *essence*, the *true being*, the spirit or soul of a human individual, 'The Floating Man', a thought experiment from a thousand years ago, is an invaluable aid. Avicenna pictures a man suspended in a darkened space, with his arms and legs splayed apart, so that he is entirely without sensation or any experience. He can see, touch, smell, hear, or taste absolutely nothing, and experiences no sense data, even of his own body. He should be aware of nothing, yet he is aware of some kind of private *being*.

Without physical experience and senses, if these solely support his vitalism and significance, (as materialism suggests), there should *be* nothing. Yet he remains aware of some sort of personal and private existence beyond these. This is clearly the private *essence or true being* that is independent of physics. Clearly, there is one thing in him that is distinct from another. A taste of this is gleaned whenever we are exposed to social isolation.

Man has choice of wilful focus of dual sort. He may choose more to focus most on sensation and *physical* experience, (or on what he perceives), or on what is *intelligible* to him by mental life and vitalism, by acts of thought apprehending what he can conceive. While both are fragments of any whole reality, what is physical is finite and in physics ends, while what is intelligible, *including* physical things of truth, is therefore unchangeable and endless. The intelligible order is the order of *all* things, (the logos), and this encompasses *all truths*, however fragmentary, even those of the sensory order.

The *logos*, and what is intelligible, requires *mind*. Mental life is what connects, channels, and mediates, between whatever has true being, (including what has physical existence, for this also is required to be true), on the one hand, and what *authorises*, on the other. This requires explanation.

If anything is to be said to exist, or to have being, (in the actual way of being *truth*), it requires provenance of origination that is something intelligible to *mind*, while at the same time being greater than any *one* human mind. The logos is the intelligible thread common to *all* things that can ever be, (of which all things anyway are composed, like a rope containing knots). This is an order of intelligibility of all that *is*, and the compatibility of the human mind is accommodated within this, so that its origin is *bound* to the logos, and thereby authorised. However, this underpinning order is clearly not the creation of any single sort of inadequate human mind.

Nonetheless, this order, or logos, supporting all that can be, by its compatibility with the nature of human minds, and *requiring* anything that can *be*, to be intelligible intrinsically, is unassailable. Without this supporting order, nothing '*is*'. In addition, the order itself smacks of intentionality and deliberation as well, for we find all individual things 'hooked' into other things.

We know no human mind is capable of such mental and creative vitality, and therefore cannot avoid the resilient and perennial prospect of a massive superior intelligible input, applied from elsewhere, and far beyond what even our own greatest minds can conceive. Even the argument of sufficient reason may pose us here with being obliged to infer from these experiences an eternal mind, that of a creator.

The intelligible, intended, and wilful order of the logos is of intellective nature. It is responsible for connecting our 'floating man' with all that has true being, in spite of his inability to access any sort of sense experience, and therefore quite independently of any physics. His 'self-being', or essence, of personalised kind, has *provenance and authorisation* in the intelligible and wilful order derived of some divine 'mind'.

By distinguishing ethics from virtues, the seen from the unseen, change from the changeless, and, not least, body from mind, we are obliged to grasp that any sensible object, *unless* underwritten by the *truth of its being*, can be nothing. It is the abstraction, (as object of truth), or self-standing entity, provides implied *substance and significance*, to all physical things. Without this they express nothing and have no claim on reality. As Parmenides would urge us to recognise millennia ago, substance in truth is changeless and unalterable and never *ceases to be*.

Enlightened by such a reasoned philosophic attitude, we are freed from the restrictive viewpoint of empiricism and pragmatism, and at liberty to countenance as entirely plausible the immortal potentiality of 'soul' or 'spirit'. After all, truth is the ongoing register of an *unchanging substance*, (an object of being), composing an entity, *however* it may express itself in physical or passing form. This represents no more than an *appearance* of something in the world. That it is at the same time an object of truth, intelligible to us, makes it clear that we can do better than merely hold to this as some unsupported belief, based on no more than opinion.

Argument and objection raised, to the prior requirement of anything that it should have true being *in order to appear* in the world, all shares to some degree the same weaknesses, faults, and errors. Unerringly truth is treated as a property or attribute *aside of* things, regarded as if it may or may not apply.

Instead, if there is appearance of something, and it is not illusion, then it is appearance as entailed by *substance or essence* originating in *true being*. At the level of appearance, question and objection is justifiable, but once appearance may be taken seriously, truth derives self-evidently from the *being* of something.

Things derived of truth whether physical or an abstract entity, owe their existence to it. Always this is missed when focus is *aside of,* or 'over the shoulder' of a thing that is actually contemplated. No such arguments seem to recognise that without truth of the sort described here to sustain them, no 'things' are possible in the first place, whatever their seeming properties may be.

Charles Peirce shares with Sartre, and many others, the misunderstanding that what actually constitutes a reality is in one way or another derivative from what can be established as intelligible *to us.* Peirce does so by his reliance on what is established or received wisdom by *consensus,* and Sartre by a somewhat capricious method of 'forming values of things as we go along in life'. All such approaches are in relation to what is *knowable,* but we have already accounted for an *intelligible being of true things* that are perfectly plausible *without* any *human knowing.* Their intelligibility may well be there *without* their being *intelligible to us.* Of all things intelligible, what may be intelligible to one individual may well *not* be intelligible to another. This does not call in question the intelligibility principle, but the aptitudes of individuals, (and collectives for that matter).

Truth is the whole and complete *realityscape* to which *all* separate or individual intelligible things are mere fragmentary beings, and always opaque to us is its totality, much as Hegel or other philosophy, even from classical times, and through Spinoza, favouring the *one,* may advise. Whether things exist or have being, they are not required to bear some 'property' of truth like a badge so to explain them, and *compelling* us, to *know* it. Neither is human knowledge so boundless that it can coalesce into any sort of inventory for us. The element of mystery always pertains in spite of advances that are made in what may be *knowable.*

Nonetheless, only if things are *of* truth, in actuality, having real *being,* can anything claim to *exist* at all. If anything is to be scrutinized, it is merely a scrutiny of *how we arrive at our belief* that truly we are encountering them. If satisfied with our approach, then are we confident that we have applied sound justification for our belief, and that things 'are', or have being, and cannot be otherwise. This always is a matter of integrity within private epistemology.

In our consideration of what is true and real, nothing may be of greater concern to us than the human individual. If we are to be more than some fictional creature, no more substantive than some flight of fancy, how far is it possible that we may feel justified to believe it, or, even more, ascertain that we can reliably *know* it? After all, unless there are grounds for belief in the *truth of things*, the appendices to follow this epilogue are meaningless. I am persuaded the answer to such a question hinges on the dominant part played in our lives by *mind*, or, as some may prefer, soul.

Certainly we consider the occurrence of human individual life to be an event, one that frequently we celebrate. Relativity teaches us that both time and distance between events will vary with the motion of the observer. But we readily recognise that there is some absolute *quantity*, (abstract weight of significance, a sort of *quantum*), independently belonging to events themselves, regardless of whether they are observed or not, or at what time or distance they may be placed from us. Much depends on how we regard this 'quantity'.

First, we cannot avoid that such a quantity *applies* to an event. For example, no distance in space, or in time, as we have seen, lessens a tragedy. In this particular case the quantity is the tragedy, though it could, as easily be anything else, such as 'joy'. The 'quantity' of a man's life is independent of any distance or period of time with which it can be associated, for it is the abstract weight of his significance that counts. This does not have shape or size in the world, (though his properties and attributes may well do so), so that none of the usual scales or measures contribute any element of additional understanding to his undeniable 'quantity', or his substance.

Secondly, as we have nothing material to aid our understanding of the 'quantity' of an event, though it has *weight in terms of significance*, (and this is an object of abstraction we can *feel*), we have no choice but to try to grasp an understanding of it in terms of the *non-material*, as it impresses on the *mind*.

We are obliged in other words to resolve the issue according to the metaphysic principle. For this mind is *required*. That this is so stems from the fact that within boundaries of physics, the three dimensions of space, and the one of time, there is no sufficiency to accommodate things of perpetuity and truth that cannot change, for change is its means of registering things. There is neither the sufficient time to support the 'always' of perpetuity, changelessness is impossible in the *motion* that time measures, nor is there any geophysical space possible to house the 'changeless'.

Giants of philosophy may comfort us, and amongst their work we may have every hope of stumbling into the finest of philosophers' 'stone'. It is entirely consistent with Plato's *appearance and reality* that we may encounter *form* and *substance* as common to one single event. The *form* we may consider the *appearance* of an event in the material circumstances of space-time of four dimensions, while the *reality* of the same event is the actual *substance*, or unseen 'quantity' of it, that we seek. Our response is to *feel* something about things, whether they are physical or not. The substance of things remains even when their physical register no longer exists.

In this regard, Aristotle would speak of the *essence* of what we contemplate, Plotinus the *soul*, Marcel the *being*, all fragments to the *truth* of which Christ speaks, and this Hegel addresses as the *absolute idea*, or the whole of all that is inclusive and one with reality. The classical world or Spinoza refer to it as the 'one', and others the 'logos', or the principle of intelligibility as I choose to present it here. This we image as the thread that substantiates all that comes into being.

The 'quantity' we seek is clearly nothing material, but the truth *substance or essence is* the thing that never ceases to be, as Parmenides puts it. The quantity or substance of events *in the world* 'appear' clothed in physical properties suitable to the *appearance* of something. These can be observed. The substance or essence of events, differently apprehendable to mind, however, and to which this appearance is 'wed', (and upon which also it depends to occur at all), requires no show of physical properties to support its true *being*. As something *beyond* physics it cannot end, but neither can it be observed. It must be apprehended differently. This requires mind.

We may use as an example the event of mind where an act of thinking is directed in contemplation upon an object of love, an object of abstraction, personified as an individual, who is the subject, or object of love, to which our thought is directed. When the object of our love, (its quantity or substance), is removed from observation by death or otherwise, the substantive object of our love is not removed also.

We may engage with this at any time of our choosing, for its ongoing being of truth does not end. The event in the *world of appearance*, death, (that we accuse of depriving us), leaves the *ongoing substance of reality*, in place, as an event of mind, and wholly unaffected. This is the meaning of the words of Adrian Henri when he can declare, 'love is what's there when you're away from me'. We have in one entity an observable *form*, and an unobservable *substance*. What is *formal* (in the sense of material presentation) ends, while what is essential or *substantive* does not. What has no end is truth, and it is this that is unchanging reality.

Apprehending the occasion of thoughts, or encountering objects of contemplation to which they refer, rightly we call mind events. *Understandings*, and what is derived from such mind events, and the events themselves, have decided *location* for mind in that it directs thought habitually and directly *upon* things, as if itself a party to that same location. If of course a human individual is a being of truth, then it is easy to see that spirit or mind, contingent on the logos or order of all intelligible truth, intrinsically is obliged to be a 'party to the whole', and is, indeed, *sharing* the location of all truth. This may be with reason conceived as the spirit world, Hegel's 'absolute idea', the 'sigma', or even the 'kingdom within' to which theology refers.

By contrast, physical, (as against mental) events, are resolutely embedded in the physical world, *in* a place, and *at* a time, and this may be refered to as *location in space*. These are distinct and contrasting locations. Mind events, though they may be shared, are essentially private, internal, and self situate in terms of mind direction. Physical events are externally and spatially situate in a *different* place or location. It is clear by this that often a mind event does not occur *in the same place* as a person, even though mind and person are one and the same identity. A ubiquitous example of this may be 'daydreaming', and another may be some nightmare where we may encounter drowning from falling from a boat.

An apple *I observe* in the physical world is in space, but an apple *I contemplate* is not. Both have location in truth always, but this cannot be ongoing in space. The apple I perceive is transitional, sharing an inner reality I apprehend and conceive as truth, (its substance), with an external life of physical dimension. The external and internal realities are separated yet inter-related. It is mental life *empowers us to distinguish the difference*, though the apple cannot do the same, lacking self-awareness. It is also this same *mental life*, (mediating by intelligibility), that distinguishes our 'floating man' from an item of beach flotsam, even to himself.

Throughout this book the central theme concerns distinguishing features of living and existing 'things' as evident by physics, and the truth being of 'things' as evident by metaphysics. As it has attributed greater import to what is *not* seen than to things that are, it is hoped that the reader is now inclined to place greater reliance on what can be *ascertained*, by making necessary connections between what we are *able* to experience, and to what extent this empowers us reasonably to infer things that we cannot.

I am persuaded that such thoughts lead ultimately to a serious appraisal of the inner human individual as a profoundly spiritual *being of truth*, of primary place, that is unchangeable, however burdened by adventures through time and space in a physical world, where all material things are bound to serial change and endings. When a man is incapacitated to the world, as by stroke or coma, like our floating man, though in time and space, he is inaccessible to the action of stimuli *to* the physical world, or *from* it. It can resemble in this way the posture of death. It is his true being that maintains a variety of personal and private existence that remains independent of contact with the sensory world.

Issues of *itness*, and consequences of it, (whether events or individual things), rest within momentum of time, expressed in 'now' moments. All of these are directed *anyway* to rest and entropy, measuring a state of no available energy, so that rest inevitably overpowers motion. 'Momentum' is a *rate of motion*, and this should not be confused with the *itness* of *what is moving* which is not the same thing.

When *itness* stops moving through physics which has 'ended', this does not require that the itness *also* is ended. Itness, truth object that is unchangeable, may *experience* 'momentum', but is distinct *from* it as an *object of truth*. Truth, its *heimat*, is always a continuum. The identity and *itness* of any *thing*, is therefore primarily recognised as the uninterrupted *being* of it, independently of any changes or endings that everywhere abound in the physical or sensory world. Always it is bound as a fragment to the whole of everything that can ever be, and it is this that comprises what may be imaged as a pan-reality.

Individually and alone, whether Caesar's apple, my dog, or me, always it is a fragment to the whole of what can be, and it is its very fragmentation from the whole that sets the boundaries of its distinction from *other* identifiable objects, each fragments themselves, of the whole of reality. Each fragmentary *itness* is the personalised *being* distinguishable from others, the total of which constitute absolute truth. Without each fragment, the whole *cannot* be complete, and therefore each is *necessary*. This is why personalised minds are highly requisite. It is also why men must value each other.

Clearly within that absolute whole of truth and reality, there are unquantifiable and unmeasurable classes and categories, and universals are our attempt to address them. That some may be unintelligible to us, or we have failed to make the necessary connections to unveil them, does not mean they are not there. Humility in the face of what presents as mystery is required.

Not all classes and categories however *are* unintelligible to us, and we are empowered by reasoning or other means, such as apperception and intuition for example, to discern that both objects of *material* and objects of *abstraction* are required items of any whole truth, and that reality is incomplete without either one of them. Clearly all distinct individual things are each *necessary*.

It follows that it is insufficient to apprehend a human individual as a lump of material only, or a collection of atoms, disposable to absolute truth. Without primary or elemental substance as a *truth object*, measurable and physical properties of material or matter, without truth-value, an individual cannot be anything. In effect we are obliged to place *being* before the secondary classification of *human*. This in turn requires the metaphysic principle to be recognised so that sufficient evaluation of the physical material can qualify it as truth being.

Matter, given to the procedure of entropy, (changes and ending), without something added to it, clearly cannot alone qualify as 'unchanging' truth. Even recorded histories, dependent on memory and *knowledge*, cannot raise matter to the condition of unchangingness that truth dispenses to it. In any case, *history relies upon being known*. As conceded already what is known does not encompass everything.

This leaves the human being as an individual with no alternative to that of *requiring* the addition of some non-material *form, essence, or meaning* that is durable, and which is independent of physics and its effects, so endowing that individual with the immutability that truth and reality require. This additional element we are obliged to identify as substance or essence, spirit or soul, or what the ancient Greek referred to as 'pneuma'.

Without this man cannot be taken seriously as a *species* of reality, never mind as an individual person. It is our intuitive and apperceptive awareness of spirit, soul, and pneuma, in individuals as truth objects, that induces us all to feel the ongoing presence of loved ones who no longer live. We are not imagining a presence, for they, like us, are issues of the metaphysic truth to which all real things are accountable including ourselves. This sensitises us with empathy for our fellows. Life and existence of physical import may be regarded as an *expression aside* of an unending *being*. After all, life and existence, without *true being*, is not possible.

I regard the convergence of all this with the substance of Christian teaching as the natural outcome of stripping away the self-grooming conceits of empiricism and passionate obstinacy of one-eyed materialism, so to unveil the *necessity* of the metaphysic principle. With the unfortunate affliction of Pinocchio, it is possible not to see what is plainly before the nose.

Beginnings and endings may be everything to physics, but are meaningless to what is always *beyond* and out of reach for them. *To be a human individual is being something, not only while existing, but more importantly, in perpetuity, for such an individual is a being of truth that never changes or ends.* Death is a phenomenon of physics alone.

With such as this in mind, I offer the reader three appendices, which, combined, make a powerful springboard for self-reappraisal of life-changing proportion. One concerns a brief synopsis of supportive philosophic attitude, another a scale of morality level, by which self-assessment may be made, (with its implications for any collective society within which we live), and yet another is the largely unpublished spirit guidance of Christ, as represented in St. Thomas' Gospel, all of which are mutually supportive.

APPENDICIES

Appendix One – Making Links

Part One – Deference to Parmenides

Advancing from Parmenides, he declares that when you think you think *of* something; when you use a name, it must be the name *of* something. Both language and thought then, require objects outside of themselves. (This should not be misconstrued as a *play* on language, but a fundamental fact of how constructs of language are to thought like an *aide de camp* to the act of thinking in support of *conceiving*). Further to this it enables communication of sometime complex ideas.

It is similar in the case of the relation between motion and phenomena; if there is motion, there is motion *of* something, and if there is phenomenon, it is *of* something. Thus we can see that motion and phenomena, (like language and thought), require objects outside of themselves to which they are reference. For motion to apply phenomena are required, and where there are phenomena there is motion. While both are aspects of physics, both require something that is *not* physics if they are to be actual, and this is authenticity and actuality of *being truth* as an entity of abstraction.

Before continuing, I must say that denial or evasion of this, attributing to language use, (as with subject-object orientation), a discrediting and built-in error of application, is perverse and absurd. Revelation, by whatever means of mental life, derived of responsible percipience and rumination, requires only sufficient articulation for the communication of the idea, (and its supporting references of self-consistent logic or reasoning), for it to be of validity and significance. That fault may rightly be found with the *articulation* of something, reflects no equal fault on the *idea* authorising it. The two are very distinct.

To return to abstraction, when we contemplate things-in-themselves, as with universal abstract entities, like beauty or whiteness it is not beauty or whiteness *of something else* we contemplate. Truth is similarly an entity of abstraction as are all actual entities open to an act of thinking or conceiving. In the case of an act of thinking directed to the *being* of a human individual, it is the object of *truth* upon which we focus, whole personhood, and not merely the part of him that mediates as an agent of physics, his big feet, teeth, his nice voice, or even his whole body.

Since you can think or speak of a thing, or contemplate it at *one time as well as any other*, (this includes human individuals), and since phenomena of true things may be also in motion in the world at one time, (or not), as well as any other, what may be thought or spoken of, or what may phenomenalise, must be relations *to something* that in some sense exists at *all* times. This is necessary so that *always* they are to be accessible, and of truth that neither changes nor ends.

Thinking, contemplating, and speaking of something requires the act of thinking prior to speaking, and this is *conceiving* or envisaging in contrast to observing and *perceiving*. Thought and speech are relations to objects outside of themselves that are *authorised* by required concepts. Motion, and phenomena of things, employs perception to apprehend them. What is apprehended these ways are *relations* attributes of *things-in-themselves*, (not objects of truth that are abstractions).

There are relations, properties or attributes *belonging* to abstract entities. This is rather like the way we may see only the proverbial 'cloud of dust' and not the thing causing it. While a required concept or *object of truth* is engaged routinely by act of thinking, or conceiving, it is *not* required that also it should be *perceived*. Required concepts are accessible only to acts of thought, beyond sensory perception.

Both acts of thinking and motion of things then, (conceiving or perceiving), require engagement with *actual* entities, however they may be mediated by relations. The thought and the motion are distinguishable from the truth objects they serve. The actuality of the entities must be of reality and *true being*, or all acts of thinking, and motion of anything, is illusory and unreal. Such entities of *essence, true being*, or *substance* of fixed identity, is clearly neither the act of thinking, nor the motion to which they are subjected, which are merely *relations* to necessary or essential things; the *essence* or *substance* of actual, though non-material things, to which relations are *added*.

The truth being of something is wholly unaffected by such things as having acts of thinking directed to them, or how motion influences their related manifestations in the physical world; to Oscar Wilde in his prison, or Milton with his own place of 'mind', always they are accessible. Relations of motion exist in the four dimensions of space and time, (these are like wind or currents of water). *Properties and relations* to a being of truth, (i.e. the essential substance or essence of a thing), are grounded in this theatre of operation. This is *life and existence* in the world.

Properties and relations are something *other* to the object of truth, and are therefore subject to motion and change, (like the leaf in wind, or the pebble in water). Space and time, while modifying the agent, (this is the clutch of properties *added* to an essential true being), also must be traversed, and for this there must be two termini, those of beginning and ending. This is quite a distinct scenario to that of the *essential being* (to which these relations and properties apply), for this pertains always, and is susceptible to nothing of the kind.

Change, (and it is time measures this), in no way modifies a truth, for as Parmenides reminds us, change consists in 'things coming into being' and 'ceasing' from *being*. How can what *is*, he asks, only be 'going to be', and how can what *is*, come into being. If it *can* come into being, he suggests, then we can be sure it is *not*, and *if* it is, (already and always), how can it be 'going to be'.

It is here we are empowered to make a necessary connection with the thoughts of Hegel, for when it comes to what *is* by its *being* of truth, Parmenides describes it as follows; the only true being, (what truly is), and *always* so, is the *one*, and it cannot be divided, (making all fragments of it necessary) because the whole of it is present everywhere wherever anything *is*.

Clearly his conception of the *whole of all truth*, and anything that ever *is*, is encapsulated by his notion of the *one*. This in meaning converges with the notion centuries later in Hegel's promulgation of the *absolute idea*, and later again, reinforces the distinction between physical and metaphysical things, in our own time, made by Gabriel Marcel with his *Etre et Avoir*, referring to *life* and *true being*.

Part Two – Deference to Hegel

Hegel claims that everything short of the whole of all things, abstract or material, is clearly fragmentary, and it cannot exist without everything else. Any individual thing he says 'hooks' into other things, (as Russell puts it), all of which combine into a hierarchical whole truth, which he describes as the *absolute idea*. Nothing has being except as a part of absolute truth. From a single bone, a scientist is empowered to infer the whole animal. Every separate piece of reality coalesces with the next, and the next, until the whole is complete. The incompleteness of individual things appears equally in the world of thought as in the world of things.

When this incompleteness of any one thing is overlooked, (idea or sense object), we run into contradictions he asserts. What *is* cannot be self-subsistent without other things, and what *is* must contain reference to those other things to *be* what it is. I regard this as highly relevant to the principle of intelligibility as the dispensation or apportioning of truth to an object of thought, or an object of thing, (as its underpinning authentication). This allows it actually to *be* anything. It is its intelligibility binds it to the order of the logos, and, however individual a thing may be, it is a party to the whole of all that truth can be. This is what Parmenides calls the *one*, and what Hegel calls the *absolute idea*.

Hence we see clearly how no thing is self-subsistent without other true things to which it must make reference, so allowing it to be the separated thing of individuation and *itness*, or identity that it is. Russell puts it that a man's nature for example is constituted by memory, knowledge, loves and hatreds, and so on. There is much more of course. But for these things, and others, he cannot be what he is.

For my own part this is insufficient, and I must add the further example that unless bound to the whole of truth, (albeit a miniscule fragment of it), such a man has no *true being*, and without this, he cannot anyway exist at all in life. Nonetheless, such a man, presented as sum total of reality, is self-contradictory. Even a buttercup is a fragment only of truth, nothing real without its relations to earth, the galaxy, and the 'big bang'. Given all this, though a portion only, of all there is, it has *being in truth*.

Many examples can be used like this to demonstrate that no *thing-in-itself* is complete without other things. Hegel claims advance may be made this way until we reach the notion, whatever may be added, of the *absolute idea*. This he says has 'no incompleteness and has no need of further development'. This absolute reality forms one single harmonious system, not in space or time, is wholly rational, and wholly spiritual. Any suggestion to the contrary in the world we know, can be shown logically says Hegel to stem from a *piecemeal and fragmentary view*, (or percept), of something greater.

If we were to see the universe whole, he adds, all striving and struggle disappears, so that seeing it as we may suppose God sees it, we see an eternal, perfect and unchanging spiritual unity, however modules of it, as separated fragments, may appear to pronounce their singularity. Time and space involve separateness and multiplicity of separate things, with even the 'now' moment separate from the next. Without the next, and the next and so on, there could be no 'now' moment. The 'now' is incomplete, just as a sphere is incomplete. It cannot be a sphere without a boundary, and something, at least empty space, within it.

A sphere cannot self-subsist unless its incompleteness is *recognised*. The incompleteness even of physics in general *requires* metaphysical substantiation and credentials, so to participate in total reality. The absolute is pure being. An individual person is not all of reality. What is real *of him* is his participation *in* reality-as-a-whole, and this is not his *life and existence*, but his true *being*, without which he would have no life, or existence, of *any* kind. *Life and existence* is merely 'an aggravated circumstance' of *true being*.

Appendix Two – Lawrence Kohlberg

Developmental Stages of Morality

This important and reliable outline of developmental stages from infancy, through adolescence, to full maturity, self-evident to any astute observer, as a dependable measure of advance to independent thinking and private and public well-being, would appear largely to be ignored by educationalists at the time of writing.

The inevitable result, to which present day society has succumbed, is that leadership of individuals from youth is misdirected to self-gratification. The lack of a sense of self-worth and significance, not to mention sense of security, with which young and old should be equipped, emerges today as the most noticeable and characteristic deficiency of society.

Unless there is renewed interest in what Kohlberg outlines, and which I reproduce here, fragmentation, dissention, and even public disorder, is the most likely outcome of individuals leading disordered lives. What history teaches us about this, is that in the field of political leadership, and especially at the hands of ultra liberal democracy, tyranny adopts the mantle of being the only route of escape from unbridled disorder.

Certainly it is the most readily obvious route of escape from the total breakdown and disorder that extreme varieties of democracy have been known to nurture, as in the time of Socrates. It is interesting to note that his life became forfeit largely as a result of his teaching against the moral laxity of the democracy in which he lived. What Kohlberg outlines would not I am sure meet with his disapproval.

The Preconventional Level of Morality

As observed in the young child, response is to cultural rules and labels of good, bad, right or wrong, but interpreted in terms of physical or hedonistic consequence to action, (punishment, reward, exchange of favours etc), or in terms of compliance according to the *physical power* of *those who enunciate* the rules and labels. There are two stages to this level.

1. **Punishment and obedience orientation**. The physical consequence of action determines its goodness or badness, *regardless* of any meanings or values associated with those consequences. Avoidance of punishment and unquestioning deference to power are valued in their own right, *not* in terms of respect for any underlying moral order supported by the 'authority'.

2. **Relative instrumentation orientation**. Right action consists of that which instrumentally satisfies ones own needs, and, occasionally, the needs of others. Human relations are viewed in terms similar to those of the market place. Elements of fairness, reciprocity, and equal sharing are present, but always interpreted in a physical and pragmatic way. Rather than a matter of loyalty, gratitude, or justice, it is more a matter of 'you scratch my back and I'll scratch yours'.

Conventional Level

This level concerns maintaining the expectations of an individuals family, group, (including today street gangs), or nation, and is perceived as valuable in its own right, *regardless* of immediate and obvious consequences. The attitude is one not only of conformity to personal expectations and social order, but also of loyalty to it, actively maintaining, supporting, and justifying, and identifying with the persons or group who are like minded. This level comprises the following stages.

1. **Interpersonal concordance *good boy, nice girl* orientation**. Good behaviour is that which pleases or helps others, and is approved by them. Conformity to stereotypical *images of what is the majority or natural behaviour* frequently judged by intentionality. He means well becomes important for the first time. Approval *earned* by being *nice*, (or in the case of street gangs, nasty enough).

2. **Law and order orientation**. Orientation towards authority, with fixed rules, and social order. Right behaviour consists in doing ones duty, showing respect for authority, and maintaining the social order for its *own* sake. (Street gangs may be said to operate their own interpretation of order).

Postconventional Level

Here there is a clear effort to define moral values and principles that have validity and application quite *apart* from the authority of the group, or other persons holding such principles, and apart also from any identification with such groups within ones own individual outlook. Gang members make this transition only with difficulty when they mature sufficiently to recognise their individuality. Again, this level has two stages.

1. **Social contract and legalistic orientation.** Right action defined in terms of individual rights and utilitarian application of criteria critically examined and agreed by the whole society. Emphasis on procedural rules for reaching consensus, accommodating an awareness of the relativism of personal values and opinions. Objectively, and quite apart from what is constitutionally and democratically agreed upon, what is right is a matter of *values* and *opinion*, but the legal point of view takes pre-eminence, with the possibility of changing it on rational grounds to accommodate considerations of social utility. This contrasts with the freezing of codes in terms of the earlier stage of development of *law and order*. Outside the legal realm, the binding element of obligation is subject only to free agreement and contract. This is said to be the official level of morality of the United States Government, and its constitution.

2. **Noumenal principle orientation.** The *right* distinguished by individual conscience, and in accord with distinctly favoured principles arrived at by self-examination, and underwriting a clinging in epistemic privacy to what is considered *goodness ;or virtue.* They may be ethical and abstract, or may incorporate divine command where this is accredited. They are principles that may incorporate also a sense of ultimate moral justice, and the hallmark of these things is an unfailing regard for the dignity of all human individuals. This level assures *self-autonomy, self-direction, and self-responsibility.*

Appendix Three – Convergence

Convergence with Christian Thought
The Testimony of Gospel Writing

Though the writings of St Thomas are omitted from the bible, his gospel has much convergence with the overall theme of ideas encountered in this book, with particular regard to metaphysics. It is for that reason that it is included as a testimony additional to the reasoning that precedes it here.

Though Bertrand Russell professed the philosophic attitude of atheist nature, his objectivity is highlighted to his credit when he declared that most of the best of Western Philosophy tends to be in agreement with Christian thinking. In view of the fact that secularist and Christian great thinkers endorse on the whole the existence of *spirit or soul* and share much under the metaphysical principle, (along with the central notion of the Orphics many centuries *before* them), it seems only reasonable that this shared concept should be taken seriously even by the reluctant cynic.

The difficulty however of offering support to the accompanying spirit of man, as illustrated on the cover of this book, is that the so-called 'Scholars Translation' of the Gospel of St Thomas is ridden with disconcerting errors of repeated translation, transcription, and interpretation through Hebrew, Greek and Latin. This is hazardous in the extreme, often presenting inconsistencies and contradictions of a capricious nature, no better exemplified than in the Line 14 of that version where it is suggested that *sin and damnation* are *no better assured than by prayer, fasting, and acts of charity.* One does not need to be a cleric to recognise the perverse misrepresentation of the teachings of Christ in such a line as that.

It is with such as this in mind that I have chosen to include these sayings of Christ more in line with expectations and intentions of their author, (his devoted follower and disciple), and with the scriptures in general. I feel it is better to do this, than to omit it altogether on account of previous mishandling, when there is clearly so much to offer in spirit that converges, and is in support of, the reasoning preceding it.

The form of *representation* I have adopted is in the cause of ease of reading, having the general appearance that one might expect of a news reporter's record of a live encounter. It should be borne in mind that it is indeed a representation, and therefore, although I have done my best to retain the spirit of intention of the original, in the light of what is extensively known of the teaching of Christ, authenticity of language is unavoidably altered though I have done my best to be faithful to the authenticity of substance conveyed. I have indicated for comparison's sake, the relevant lines in the left hand column tabulating the line-by-line progress of the gospel.

A reappraisal of the Gospel of St. Thomas

1. Whomsoever apprehends fully what I say to you shall never taste death.

2. Those who feel they should seek should not stop until they find. When they do find, they will find also that it is life changing, for finding a truth erases all previous unfounded beliefs and misconceptions. Then they have peace and rest.

3. If your leaders say to you Heaven, Paradise, the Father's Kingdom, is in the sky, then the birds will be there before you. If they say it is in the sea, then it is the fish that are there. The kingdom is *beyond* such things, *yet* it is within you. Knowledge of yourself is your path to wisdom and to God. You will come to understand you are merely children of the Father of all life, and not fully to know yourself in this way is true spiritual poverty.

4. The aged, who do not fail to inspire the young with the significance of life, and pass on their enthusiasm for truth, will not fail to realize their own eternal life. Whether great or small in our engagement with spiritual life, each of us shares in it regardless.

5. By your love and sincerity, in all your doings with the external world, the light within you will become clear to you and your fellows. Most of all it is clear to the Father, for nothing, however hidden from this world will go unnoticed.

6. The disciples asked Jesus if he wanted them to fast from things, in what manner they should pray, whether they should give to charity, and was

there any particular diet he could recommend. His reply surprised them, for He told them 'do not lie, even to yourself, and do nothing that inwardly you despise. Nothing is ultimately hidden, and what you feel and do does not go unobserved'.

7.   He told them that as lions and humans are distinguishable in that humans are spiritual beings, so too is flesh just as distinguishable from spirit.

8.   He urged them to employ discretion in life's choices, like the wise fisherman, who drew in his net full of small fish, but amongst which he discovered a large one. The fisherman gave all the small fish back to the sea but retained the large one. The wise individual should conduct his life likewise, using discretion in what he encounters.

9.   He told them the story of the sower going out with a handful of seeds, scattering them. Some reached the road, where birds gathered them up. Others fell on rock with no fertile soil for them to take root, while others fell among thorns that could only stint their growth. But those that fell on good ground ultimately produced a good crop. All that is necessary is provided for the discriminating mind.

10. Though He had set the world ablaze, he told them, its ultimate consummation is an ending of benevolence under His ever-present guardianship. (This is intended to inspire confidence).

11. Any heaven they experience, or any that they image, He reminded them, are things that pass, for they must submit to what is actual ultimately. This parallel is discernible in life and death. On the day their *spirit* was created *already* they were *one* with what *is actual*, but with their body added, he told them, they became in a sense two. Dead things you eat have life within you, He told them, though they are not all there is of you. Life should be conducted accordingly.

12. His followers asked Him next that as they knew they could expect Him to be leaving them, to whom should they then look for guidance and leadership. He replied to this that with His presence no longer a thing of life, they were to be guided by that truth for which both heaven and earth were brought into existence. (We are left to suppose or infer that this is the *expression* of benevolent love and wisdom that is the *very fabric of the creation* itself).

13. He asked them to compare their image of Him, as they understood Him, with something with which already they were familiar. Peter compared Him with a messenger, Matthew a philosopher, and Thomas, a teacher. Thomas added that in spite of this, truly he felt utterly incapable of comparing Him with anything. Jesus said to Thomas that He was no teacher, yet though He had tended and nurtured what was already within them all, this had made it difficult for them to compare Him adequately with anything, rendering them speechless. It was at this point that He took Thomas aside and spoke privately to him. Of course on Thomas returning to his companions they wanted to know what Jesus had said to him. Though he would not tell them, we are left to assume that Jesus was somewhat pleased with Thomas, and that if Thomas had communicated this to his fellows, it may have induced some sort of envy. We may assume this readily in that Thomas did say to his companions that if he were to tell them, they would stone him.

14. Jesus told them that even in fasting, prayer, and being charitable, there is opportunity for sin where motivation for these things are impure as when something gainful is in mind. He advises to *be* just as *seen* to be, with pure intention, and to do good only that stems from this, for this is what defines sincerity of character. While what goes into the mouth does not defile, what comes out of it often does so.

15. *Quantum life* itself, (weight of significance or *essence*), is not born of woman, and wherever this is encountered, (even within the private self), what is encountered is the *giver* of life, the creator Father.

16. He told them there are those who imagine that He has come into the world to *impose* peace and rest and that this is a misunderstanding. He does not dictate these things and conflict must inevitably arise.

17. Even houses will divide, father against son and son against father, but as this is self-will, each will be accountable. In quantum life or essence what He does bring is love and life that is beyond the appreciation of senses alone.

18. They asked Him then how was their *end* to come, and he chastened them with His reply. He said that as they were contemplating some kind of end, they must have been presupposing some kind of *beginning*. He told them the end is precisely where the beginning is found. What *always* is truth is perpetuity, eternity, what always *is*, and this is not a thing that harbours beginnings or endings. Everything ultimately lies with spiritual awareness, and those who

have this know to what everything is orientated, and *in* what all things end, for it is where *all* things begin also. There is no *start or finish* to spiritual *being*.

19. He told them no one can begin if already they are. When they cannot truly begin, however are they to end at all. Beginnings and endings are found only in the sensory world of physics. While conscious living primarily engages itself with this, it is not all there is. Awareness of this gives you domination even over stones, which then must serve you. Eternally there are five trees supportive of spiritual being, knowing no seasons and losing no leaves. These are perpetual truths, (the virtues), accessible by intuition, that give everlasting *form* to conscious, responsible, and personalised conduct.

20. The disciples then wanted some description of what they called the kingdom of Heaven. What they were given was not a description of a *place* at all, but more a description of a *state of mind at peace.* He described it as an insignificant seed falling to prepared ground, (an unseen and creative *force* to which sensitised nutrients rush naturally and eagerly), developing into a glorious plant that is 'shelter to the birds of the sky', (encompassing every single fragment of created things inherent to the *one* of which they are a part). (This 'plant' presents imagery of absolute wholeness, completion, and resolution; a haven of peace and rest).

21. Mary asked Jesus what his disciples were like. He told her they were like children in a field they knew was not theirs, and when the owner demanded his field of them, with all willingness they would go with nothing and return it to him. He told her they were aware of their landlord, God. For this reason also were they aware of the thievery of false landlords so that they resist their theft of what is truly God's. He told her she would do well to emulate them in defending truth. When ultimate justice is finally delivered, it is to be sudden as if by a sharpened sickle.

22. As He watched babies being nursed, He told His disciples they were like those who reach God's kingdom, which prompted them to ask if they would reach it as babes. He told them that it is when the spiritual is truly married to the physical, so much that each is indistinguishable, that then, like such babes, there is undenied access to Paradise.

23. Whether an individual is chosen singly, as one from a thousand, or two from ten thousand, all will stand as one fulfilled in absolute wisdom.

24. They asked Him to show them where He resides in this wisdom, and He

told them there is a light within a person of light that shines for the whole world, adding that where this is not the case, there is darkness only. (Where there is no virtue and wisdom there is no light).

25. He advised them to nourish love in their friends, cherishing them as they do their soul, protecting them like the pupil of their eye.

26. Often He told them they recognise the fault in others, but before they can see this like the splinter in an eye, truly, they must first remove the larger one from their own eye.

27. He advised that if they gorged themselves on the pleasures of conscious life in the world, and did not fast from them where appropriate, they would never join with their Father creator.

28. Jesus told them He had made His stand in the flesh in the midst of the world, and had found many drunk with little thirst for Him. His soul ached for the children of humanity for so many were blind in their hearts. Coming into the world empty they seek to depart from it the same way. (A life entirely devoted to the senses is a life wasted).

29. With the miracle of spirituality underwriting life as it does, how greater a miracle it would be for the degenerative human body to underwrite spirituality. The flesh counts for nothing, yet how marvellous it is that such a wretched material thing can play host to such eloquence.

30. All awareness's of God he declared reduce to the *one*, and He made it clear the one is accessible through Him.

31. He said that it was not common for God to be readily recognised in things so close to home that they are familiar, in the same way that familiarity may hamper the prognosis of doctors with whom patients are familiar.

32. A city built high and in full view, and well fortified, he said, cannot fall easily, but neither is it easily hidden.

33. Spiritual awareness and wisdom should not be hidden, but like a lamp, should stand where it gives the best light.

34. Where a blind person leads another both finish in a ditch, He told them.

35. A strong and determined righteous will is not readily overcome, He advised, and this is how all should be.

36. He told them not to spend sleepless nights in anxiety, or to dwell on troubles as to where the next meal comes from, or what clothes are to be worn, for even the lilies in a field are provided for and they are never so precious as is every human individual to God. Can any garment, He asked, contribute anything to one so precious to the Father of all.

37. The disciples asked Him when He most is likely to appear to them, and when they best expect to see Him, and He told them *that* was most likely when they were in their nakedness, trampling all trappings and affections under foot, like little children. Then is it best, they were told, that they perceive the son of the living God, and without all those pretences, they then have no fear.

38. He told them that often they will feel a need to depend on the things he tells them, and there may be no one else from whom they may have such reassurances, but though craving His presence, and even if unable to find Him, His word (and/or promise), will always remain to comfort them.

39. He reminded them there would be those who would obstruct their way to Him, alienating them from Him, and barring those who *would* be with Him. He advised them to be guided by love and to hold to their tryst with Him, so avoiding such men as that.

40. He said of such men that their grapevine had been planted well away from the Father and Holy Spirit, but that having no foundation or strength in *truth* inevitably it must perish of its own accord.

41. Possessed with faith and love in their tryst, followers will be given more, while those with little or nothing of this, even of that ultimately will be deprived.

42. He advised followers to be unaffected by men of little faith, and whatever happens, even in the face of trial, they should hold fast to their tryst.

43. His disciples challenged Him on this, asking who He should be to say such authoritive things to them that should give them such hope, (and this is a form of faith). He simply responded that having given them so much that was to themselves so meaningful, how they could have such difficulty recognising Him that they should come to ask such a question. It seems, He told them, that you are so enthralled and captivated by trees, that you fail to recognise the substance of wood from whence they derive form.

44. He told them that culpable ignorance or blasphemy against the Father may be forgiven, as indeed may that against the Son of the Father, but that involving the denial of Holy Spirit is irreversible alienation that cannot be forgiven in Earth or Heaven.

45. In the same way He told them grapes cannot be harvested from thorn trees, nor figs from thistles, evil persons produce wickedness, while from overflow of the heart in good persons, good emerges.

46. Though no one is considered greater than John the Baptist, He said, yet he, who becomes a child in recognition of the kingdom, in humble submission, becomes even greater than John.

47. He said that no one person can mount two horses nor bend two bows, and it is so that no slave may serve two masters. Neither, He said, does one have the palate immediately to drink young wine after tasting of the old. Young wine may break old wineskins, while old wine spoils in new ones. An old patch is not sown to a new garment. (What is contemplated is intolerant of the spurious).

48. Sincere love is of such force that should two in the same house make peace with each other they move mountains.

49. He said that the faithful who are abandoned and left alone easily find the kingdom, for from it they come and to it they must return.

50. He told His followers that should ever they be asked where they have come from, they should explain they have come from the light that came into being of itself, and that they are merely an image created by the light. They are not themselves the light, but children of it, and the chosen of the living Father. If asked what evidence there may be of the Father in them, they should say that the answer to that lies with *motion and rest*. (True distinction between physics and what is beyond them).

51. They asked Him what was the nature of rest to which the dead had proceeded, and the spirit world that was to come, and He told them what they thought they had to look forward to pertains already within them, though they knew it not.

52. They then told Him they knew of twenty four prophets in Israel who had anticipated His coming into the world, and He reminded them that their object of contemplation should be more His presence among them, and not those now dead who merely prophesised His coming.

53. On a matter of dogma they enquired as to whether circumcision as currently socially regarded was of natural or spiritual significance or necessary, and He told them that were it so, the Father would provide that children would be born from the mother already circumcised. True spiritual gain is made by spiritual intention.

54. However otherwise impoverished, those with good spiritual intention are those who inherit the kingdom of Heaven.

55. He added that single mindedness in the love of God, even to the exclusion of father, mother, brother or sister, should be of prime motivation. Those who carry their cross as He does, He told them, are worthy of Him and the truth of His testimony.

56. He told them knowing the world is to know of death, but neither the world nor its death are worthy of any being of truth, any human individual.

57. Spirituality and the kingdom is approached prudently and cautiously, He reminded them, illustrating this as a form of discrete husbandry. When a good gardener plants good seed, He told them, if an enemy were to visit in the night planting weed amongst them, he doesn't have them pulled right away for fear of disturbing the good plants, for he knows that when the shoots grow the weeds will be so conspicuous as easily to be pulled and destroyed.

58. He added that it is only with great care and industry, withstanding harshness and difficulty, that it is possible for nourishing spiritual life to be realised.

59. He advised they should look to what is of God and the spirit within them while they live, or they may die never having satisfied their natural need of Him.

60. He remarked on the sight of a Samaritan man carrying a lamb on the way to Judea, and they said to Him that the man was doing that only to kill and eat it. He responded that the man was hardly able to eat it alive, but only after it had become a carcass. This was the way of life in the world; there is an inevitable ending to sensory life, and submission to truth and reality. Before His followers should themselves be consumed by spiritual reality, they should resolve themselves He told them, with equanimity, so to recognise at once their true standing as spiritual entities, and not divert themselves with such things as the dying or ending of the physical world.

61. He told them that of two reclining on a couch, one might die while the other may live. If He were to visit such a couch where may recline some proud individual, like Salome, she may well rebuke Him asking who He should think He is that He should be so free with her. His reply to her, He told His followers, would be that He was the one coming from the whole, the absolute, and from the Father creator nothing was denied Him. It is only by being party to the whole of the Father that one can be filled with light, He said to them, and where this is not so there is only darkness.

62. All those to whom He discloses these mysteries, He told them, are worthy of receiving them as true beings and party to the one, which He discerns.

63. He then told them a story of a rich man who invested his wealth in sowing, reaping and planting, so that he could fill his storehouses with produce and lack for nothing in the future. This was his hearts most cherished desire. In that very night he died.

64. He gave them another, saying that a man was receiving guests. Having prepared a lavish dinner, he sent his slave with the invitations. The first intended guest returned the message that as some merchants who owed him money were visiting him that very night, he would have to be excused. The second claimed to have bought a house and had no time to attend. Another claimed his friend was about to be married so that he could not come, and yet another that having invested in property he had his rents to collect. Returning to his master the slave reported all this to him, whereupon he was instructed then to go into the streets and invite any who would come. Those who do not prioritise their spiritual needs, Jesus told His followers, will find no place with my Father.

65. Yet another tale He used was of a man who owned a vineyard and rented it to some farmers. They were to work the crop, but deliver it to him. When the slave was sent to collect the crop, they beat him within an inch of his life. Thinking these people were labouring under some misunderstanding, the man sent a different slave to them whereupon they beat him also. Certain that his own son would command appropriate respect, the man sent him to the farmers. However, having grabbed him also, the farmers went further and killed him. There is no fathomable limit to evil.

66. Jesus pointed out to His followers that there were unlimited possibilities in the most unexpected circumstances, by telling them that of stones

rejected by builders, it was possible to make a keystone.

67. This and other things demonstrates how often those who so often pronounce knowledgably on things are confused and ill informed.

68. This can lead to persecution and hatred sometimes of the wise He told them.

69. He said that those spiritually aware and knowing the Father, and even the humblest simple soul guided by his heartfelt love for Him, though hungering for justice, ultimately are promised their fill of it. (A promise of ultimate justice).

70. He told His followers to bring forth what is within them already, for the spirit within them is sufficient for all needs. If there were not this within you, He promised, all would end for them with death.

71. He told them that the spirit within them is something no other can build within them but the Father.

72. A person came to Jesus seeking his intervention, asking Him to tell his brothers to divide what is their father's with him. He did not expect the reply he received. 'I am not a divider.'

73. He told His followers that spreading this wisdom required much industry for few workers, and it should be done with alacrity.

74. He likened it to many in need of slaking their thirst at the well that was empty.

75. He told them many stand at the door of this wisdom, but only the 'spirit wise' will be those who enter.

76. He added that the grail of the spirit was like the pearl that a merchant found in a delivery of merchandise. Retaining the pearl, happily he sold on the merchandise. He urged His followers to conduct themselves likewise, and to pursue only the enduring treasure within them that survives beyond the destruction of moth or worm.

77. Jesus declared unequivocally to His followers, 'I am the light that is over all things. I am everything. It is from Me that all things come forth, and it is to Me that all things attain. Split a log, I am there, lift a stone, and you will find Me there.'

78. He told his followers they travelled about to hear from and be with something as ephemeral as a reed shaken by the wind. What they perceive is not someone adorned in fine and soft robes like their rulers or those who are powerful. Certainly, He told them, they are in fine clothes, but have no notion of truth.

79. A woman in the crowd called out to Him what a fortunate womb and breasts gave such as He life, but He told her it was really fortune where those, hearing the word, resolved truly to hold to it. He told her that wombs and breasts could lead to as much misery and cries as easily as otherwise, while holding to the faith in spirit leads to no such thing.

80. He said that whomsoever comes to know the world discovers things and bodies, but of he who discovers it, is itself unworthy.

81. While it may be those with wealth who reign, He declared, it is those with true power that have no need of it.

82. He declared that whomsoever may be near Him is close to the fire, while whoever is far from Him is far also from the kingdom.

83. He said that images are clear enough in themselves, but what underwrites them is the light of the Father, and it is this renders significance to images. Though the Father is disclosed in all things, this is so neither in terms of an image nor in the light that comes from Him.

84. He commented when people are happy enough with their likeness in an image, are they equally content with the more subtle images of this other light, where, though not publicly seen in the same way, must endure forever.

85. Adam, (the first man of legend), originated from great wealth and power, He said to His followers, but was unworthy of you in his lack of wisdom and spirit that can only lead to death. Had he been worthy of you He told them, then he could not know death.

86. He told them beasts have their dens, and birds their nests, but man has no such place to lay his head. Man's place of rest issues from his mind.

87. Misery and wretchedness comes of reliance on bodies He said, for it is a body depending on a body, and how wretched a spirit or soul that depends on these.

88. He told them that in what they may seem to be, they will only feel deficient and unworthy when prophets unveil what really they are.

89. It is the potter who makes the outside of the cup for which there is much care and admiration, but he cannot but make the inside also.

90. He comforted his followers with the remark 'Come to Me, for what I demand of you is for your own comfort, and My lordship over you is a gentle one. With Me always you will be at rest and ease'.

91. They said to Him that they would like dearly to examine precisely the nature of God in Him. He answered that how oddly they could examine and study the heavens and earth so astutely; yet not know the one always in their very presence.

92. He reminded them of the necessity of their seeking until they find, and that although in the past He had not always told them what they wanted to know, yet now He is willing to tell them, they have stopped seeking.

93. He said that sacred and holy insight and wisdom is not for squandering on animals for it to come to rest in a manure heap, and that it is inappropriate to 'cast pearls before swine' in such a way.

94. But searching minds that come to knock at the door of wisdom will not find the door unopened.

95. 'If you have money', He said, 'rather than lending from it at a rate of interest, give it to those who are unlikely to repay you'. (Where their need is greater than thine you may be an agent of God's grace and this is true charity and goodness).

96. He said that the Holy Spirit and the kingdom of the Father is like the dough made by a woman in that she will split it into many loaves.

97. Or again, He told them, like a full jar of meal a woman carries, which, cracked without her notice, spills meal along the road. (Nothing of the spirit or of virtue is ever truly lost, for it is absolute).

98. Whatever the visible outcome of conflict with an evil person, ultimately it is the sword of justice of the kingdom of the Holy Spirit that assuredly brings final and ultimate justice.

99. At one point the disciples announced to Him that His brothers and mother

were standing outside, to which He replied that they, those present, along with those outside, are also His brothers and mother, in that they do what His Father expects of them; that it is such as these that enter His Father's kingdom.

100. Showing Jesus a gold coin, they complained to Him that the Emperor's people demanded taxes from them, but He told them to give to the Emperor what was the Emperor's, just as they should give to God what was His, adding they should give also to Himself what was His own.

101. He advised them both to love their mother and father, while being capable of turning from them, as indeed He Himself was so doing, but if they were truly to be His disciples, they must love their mother and father, as indeed also did He.

102. He told them it is the imprudent and unwise that, careless of their spiritual purpose, are like dogs sleeping in a cattle manger while their herds are untended.

103. He told them the prudent are blessed in that they anticipate dangers and prepare their resources for their way ahead.

104. The disciples decided independently that it was time for them to pray and fast, so that Jesus was compelled to remind them of their place. He reminded them with an analogy that it is appropriate that the groom should already have left the bridal suite before his guests pursue their private interests.

105. As the Father in Him are one, He showed them, so is it that there is no mother without the father, for they are one in their child.

106. It is when two are made one, He taught, that there are then true 'children of Adam'.

107. The benevolence and love of the Father he likened to a man with a hundred sheep, the largest one of which went astray. His attention he focused on the one lost until he found it, leaving the ninety-nine to chance. On alleviating his anxiety by finding the lost sheep, he declared his love and care for it had been greater than for the ninety-nine.

108. He told His followers that whoever assimilated His teaching fully, (drinking in His words), would become very like Him, and then, like He Himself, would find everything revealed and clear.

109. Men discovering they are Spirits of the Father's kingdom can be likened, He told them, to the story of a person who has hidden treasure in his field of which he really knows nothing. Dying, he left it to his son, who knew nothing of it either. The son sold on the field to a man who went ploughing, so discovering the hidden treasure. This is life-changing empowerment.

110. The wisest action of those with celebrity and wealth in the world is that they come to see it for the paltry thing that it is.

111. He told them both the heavens and the earth must reach an ending that obliterates all material things, but in the spirit of truth that is of the Father, ending and death is unknown. 'Have I not advised you all', said Jesus, 'those who truly find themselves discover *for* themselves that the world is unworthy of them in that their presence in it is not all there is of them'.

112. The flesh and the soul are entirely distinct and bear no resemblance to each other. Flesh entails soul or evolves from it no more than does soul evolve from flesh. They are independent of one another, so that each human individual is *two* in one.

113. His followers were then anxious to know that with the passing of the heavens and earth 'rolling up' their presence, when finally would the spiritual kingdom arrive. They were told 'It does not come by watching for it, or looking here, or looking there. Though unseen, the kingdom already runs throughout and is spread across and beyond the earth'.

Recommended Further Reading

A History of Western Philosophy   Bertrand Russell
First published 1946

Etre et Avoir   (Having and Being)   Gabriel Marcel
First published 1935

Dialogue of Comfort Against Tribulation   Thomas More
Composed in the Tower 1534

The Problems of Philosophy   Bertrand Russell
First published 1912

Authors Testament

What matters above all things to me is nothing whatever to do *with* me, my existence, destiny, or fate, but something greater than all this; that the truth I contemplate is a sufficient approximation of what is actual. Given this is so, (and by all portion of my reasoning, discernment, apperception and intuition, I have every expectation that it is so), then I am content grasping the universe, and all beyond it, as a vast harmony and unity of benevolent origin that is unending.

I am utterly persuaded of an eternality that is required of all things and all thought, that rests in the one palm of a loving creator. In such a scenario, where all separate things are necessary, cohesive, and derived as they are of His will alone, there is nothing to fear. All that is required of humans is *submission to the liberty of spirit* within them that removes all temporal and spatial chains of impediment.